ALBERT

AND THE BELGIANS

ALBERT, KING OF THE BELGIANS

ALBERT

AND THE BELGIANS

PORTRAIT OF A KING

by

CHARLES D'YDEWALLE

WILLIAM MORROW & COMPANY

NEW YORK   MCMXXXV

ALBERT AND THE BELGIANS

Translated from the French by
PHYLLIS MEGROZ

92
A333

To

GEORGETTE

FOREWORD

THIS book is not a history: it is a sheaf of memories.
As a journalist, I was often admitted into King
Albert's intimate circle, and so was able to hear his own
opinions from his own lips. Long before he met his
death, I used to marvel at the great figure of my King.
I have not sought inspiration in written texts. In future years, historians will write the life of Albert I from
documentary evidence, but my only evidence has been
the spoken word; I knew the witnesses, the hundreds of
witnesses, of the Epic. Many of them are dead; very
few have set down their thoughts. The Belgians are
not given to writing, either because of their innate reserve or from some indefinable sense of fear. It would
seem as if the watchword of the Belgian Kings, "Burn
everything . . ." has been obeyed to the letter.

King Albert loved to be made the recipient of confidences; he himself revealed his thoughts to a chosen
few. He showed no sign of his feelings to his Ministers,
yet he became expansive in the company of scholars,
writers, travellers, and his humbler subjects. My long
association with this *milieu* taught me to understand
his greatness. We loved and admired our King long
before a tragic destiny cut short his amazing life. This
book is a testimony of our devotion.

Many of those who shed light on my researches were
the victims of those incomprehensible changes of mood
which led the King to shun or misunderstand his truest

friends. I myself did not go scatheless. Historians will
not find the key to his character in text-books; and in a
quarter of a century those who hold the clue will have
relinquished it forever.

You must picture a very young man, who was so insignificant that the great ones of the earth talked freely
in his presence. You must picture him listening eagerly
to their words, and memorizing them all. The journalist who can use his eyes and ears and set a seal on his
lips, will soon acquire a unique knowledge of men.
Bismarck had a sneaking admiration for Blowitz, the
special correspondent of the *Times,* and at every important conference, he would lift the green cloth and
say sardonically: "Blowitz is not under the table . . .
we can begin." Kings, Princes, generals, and statesmen
meet in conference throughout the pages of this book.
Again I say, let no one look for documentary evidence.
There was only an unseen witness hidden beneath the
table, listening and taking notes. To-day he is publish-
ing them. He did not become a journalist until 1928,
but many of the veterans have unwound the thread of
their memories for him.

May all my readers realize that this book in its simple sincerity has been a labour of love. My gratitude
goes out to all who have honoured me with their confidence; those officers, statesmen, Colonial Governors,
diplomats and professors, who have generously aided
me in my task.

My thanks are also due to Madame Marie Gevers and
Mademoiselle Denyse Clairouin, at whose suggestion
this book was written. But for their encouragement,

I should never have ventured to weave into a pattern all these memories and impressions. In conclusion, I should like to thank my good friends, Jacqueline Lechat and Henri D'Ursel, who carefully checked my manuscript and rectified my mistakes. May all those who helped me find their reward in the knowledge that they are perpetuating the memory of one of the noblest and most beautiful characters that the world has known.

C. D'Y

April 1, 1935.

CONTENTS

ILLUSTRATIONS

ALBERT
AND THE BELGIANS

CHAPTER I

FAMILY TREE

THE Hapsburg dynasty had reigned over the Belgians for two hundred years. In the great cities of Flanders, at the close of the eighteenth century, the Flemish nobility had forgotten Flemish. The race, however, possessed extraordinary vitality; the people were poor, always ready to emigrate, and so prolific that they flowed into the armies, colonies and factories of the Great Powers. For centuries the Powers in question had agreed not so much to share Belgium amongst them as to use her for barter and for a battleground. No other country had seen so long a list of battles won by the leaders of every coalition.

At the beginning of the nineteenth century, geographers defined Belgium as the *Middle Country* and strategists called her the *Country of the Marches*. But the statesmen of 1814 alluded to her rather more crudely with the words: *Increase in Territories*. After the Battle of Waterloo there followed fifteen years of annexation to Holland.

In the spring of 1831 the Belgians, having freed themselves from the Dutch yoke, asked Prince Leopold of Saxe-Coburg-Gotha to free them also from the intrigues of the Powers—and in particular from those of Prince Talleyrand—by becoming their King. Not without some hesitation the Prince accepted.

3

The Saxe-Coburgs come of ancient and illustrious stock, but their early history shows them continually at war amongst themselves. Indeed this was only natural, for it was the essence of Richelieu's policy. The disintegration of Germany was a principle of the Balance of Power in Europe; a principle held by Charles V.

All the Saxon princes are descended from a common line of the lords of Wettin on the Saale, on the borders of Saxony and Thuringia. These rulers adhered to the practice of dividing their possessions amongst their male descendants, which of necessity weakened them. But a day came when the principal branch (the Albertine) grew more powerful than the second, the Ernestine branch. The Albertine branch of Saxony gave Poland many of her kings, and in 1806 it gave one to itself.

Meanwhile, by establishing the principle of primogeniture, the Ernestine branch had continued to flourish, though in a far more restricted area. Leopold was the eighth of the nine children of Duke François of Saxe-Coburg-Gotha. He was the youngest son of the youngest branch, and times were hard. His mother, before her marriage, had been Augusta Sophia of Reus Eberdorf; and although her fortune had been inconsiderable, she came of an illustrious family. She was not the Grand Duchess of Gerolstein, but Offenbach might have peopled his operetta from among her entourage. It was one of those comfortable little German courts where every man had to make his own way.

Between Berlin and Vienna the Coburgs had managed to develop. They had even gone as far afield as St. Petersburg, and it was there that the fortunes of the

House were secured. Julie, the eldest daughter, married Constantine of Russia. Antoinette married Alexander of Württemberg, who was then serving in the Russian army. Ernest endeavoured to make a career in Berlin. Ferdinand became an officer in the Austrian Cavalry. Leopold fell to Julie's charge. He was made a captain in the Ismailovski regiment when he was seven, a colonel when he was eight, and a general when he was twelve. The sisters in Russia had not forgotten their youngest brother.

Decidedly, the Coburgs knew how to help one another. It was one of their principles that no son of the House (with the exception of the eldest) should stay in their own province of Coburg, there to augment the crowd of idle princelings who grew fat on ecclesiastical revenues. It behoved them to be as European, as little German, as possible. So they were polyglot. Also, no money must be spent. This need for economy very soon led to a taste for economizing. They could all make minute calculations in their heads; they were careful not to expend an unnecessary louis; yet their thriftiness forsook them when it came to a question of putting their own millions at the disposal of the State.

Leopold had little formal education, but he somehow learnt everything, including music and mechanics. When he was sixteen, it was obvious that the youthful officer was firmly resolved to make his own way, despite all vagaries of fortune. His regiment of Horse Guards, commanded by his brother-in-law, Constantine, fought at Austerlitz. He himself and his brother Ernest were in the Moravian army. In 1806, Duke François died,

and was succeeded by his son, Ernest. The two young men realized the precariousness of their fortune. They had no revenue, and their military career was entirely dependent upon the good-will of the Czar.

The two brothers went to France in 1809. "I consent to their going," wrote their mother, "although my heedless Leopold is so young." In her *Memoirs of Josephine*, Mademoiselle Ducret describes him as "very boyish-looking, extremely handsome and exceedingly shy. He was sweet-tempered. I saw him nearly every day, and was impressed by the simplicity of his manners." Josephine paid him marked attention, and Hortense soon numbered him amongst the habitués of Malmaison. The Empress put her box at the Opera at the young Prince's disposal. "He was the handsomest young man I ever saw at the Tuileries," notes Napoleon in his *Memoirs* written at St. Helena. In 1812, Leopold again visited Dresden. In 1814, he had once more joined the Russian army, and during the year he paid a second visit to Malmaison.

In 1814, Princess Charlotte of England was to have married the son of Wilhelm I of Holland, who had newly been proclaimed "Heir Apparent to the Belgian Provinces"—although these same provinces had never even been consulted. This proposed union pleased the Czar, but was distasteful to the Princess herself. Aware of this, Alexander cast round for a suitor more to her liking, and mentioned Prince Leopold. The engagement was officially announced in January, 1816. The handsome Prince of Coburg received a field-marshal's baton, and was created Duke of Kendal, a title he never

assumed; for a mistress of George I, of dubious memory, had been sole titular of that duchy.

The young Prince could hardly have aspired to a happier fate, in spite of the fact that he had the Regent for his father-in-law and George III for his grandfather. In addition, there were seven uncles who were ill-disposed to him. As for his mother-in-law, Princess Charlotte said: "My mother is a wicked woman, but she would not have been if my father had not been even more wicked than she. . . ." The Archduke John described the Queen-presumptive of England in the following words: "She is young and pretty, with a good figure, and the manners and gestures of a man. . . . She is clever and well-informed, her conversation is witty, she bubbles over with high spirits, and is astoundingly plain-spoken. She seems to have good intentions, but has always done exactly as she liked, and has never been educated to be the First Lady in England. She is an extraordinary mixture. . . ."

The marriage was happy; and in due course an heir was expected. The baby was stillborn. Its mother died a few days later. Everything was over. One short year, and joy had folded its wings forever.

Leopold was reduced again to the rank of prince without a kingdom. In 1837, the daughter of the Duke of Kent, an eighteen-year-old girl, became Queen of England under the name of Victoria; and sixty years later she had not relinquished her long lease of power. In 1830, however, her uncle Leopold had been sounded by the Greeks, who were looking for a king. On the advice of Dr. Stockmar, his counsellor, the Prince post-

poned his reply. A year later, the Belgians asked him to be King.

Leopold was well aware of the situation of Belgium on the chessboard of Europe. A long initiation in British politics had enabled him to judge its worth. The Foreign Office, he knew, would be unperturbed so long as neither France nor Germany took possession of the Scheldt. He was wise enough to take advantage of the excellent opportunity the Belgians were offering.

It was July 17, 1831, when Leopold's cavalcade, coming by the road from Calais, arrived at Adinkerke in Western Flanders. Adinkerke is a village close to Dunkerke, and does duty as a frontier station between Belgium and France. It is about one and a half miles from the sea, and near the hamlet of La Panne. Leopold's carriages had been escorted by a squadron of French cuirassiers ever since they had left Calais. When the procession reached the frontier the squadron wheeled about, and a platoon of Belgian civic guards, who wore the black cockade—they were tall, red-faced young men from Brabant—presented arms. The frontier station of La Panne boasted a small inn, half tavern, half posting-house; a one-storeyed building with a red roof. Here Leopold I rested, received the congratulations of the local authorities, and then resumed his journey to Ostend. He had brought a service of English plate with him in his carriage. It was the only relic of his old life that he took to the new.

Thus the King set foot in his new kingdom. On the way to Ostend, his carriages drove across a wooden bridge which spanned a small river, one of those slow

water-courses that flow lazily through green plains. It was the Yser. . . . That day the history of the Belgian monarchy began.

A year later, at Compiègne, he married the charming Princess Louise of France, who had been known until then as Mademoiselle de Blois. She was the daughter of Louis-Philippe, who was far-seeing enough to give his consent. Thus Leopold once again attained the position for which destiny had seemed to intend him, although this time there was not quite the same element of romance.

Throughout his country, which extended from the North Sea to the forests of the Eiffel, the new King found great devotion and an equally great lack of discipline; an ardent desire for power, and an instinctive distrust of those in power. In official Belgium, he discovered a fundamental love of industry heightened by profound faith. His subjects, in short, were the best and most difficult of people. Meanwhile, he diplomatically married his niece Victoria to his nephew, Albert of Saxe-Coburg-Gotha; and it is hard to say which calls for the more admiration: Leopold's knowledge of Europe which now at last he could use in his own interests, or his art of never antagonizing those around him.

The work of education in the new régime lasted for thirty years. "They are quite unversed in politics," said the King to Lord Burnham; and when he had scrutinized the ultra-liberal text of the Constitution, he added: "Obviously, the Monarchy was not present to defend itself. . . ." The Monarchy, however, subse-

quently took its revenge, but in so discreet a manner
that no trouble arose; and so the country prospered.

From 1830 to 1870, when the young states that had
broken loose from the chains of the Congress of Vienna
were trying to maintain a foothold in Europe and were
claiming their place in the sun, Leopold I was the
Mentor King, typifying very Old Europe in his experience, and very New Europe in his advanced political
outlook.

Leopold II, however, was an absolute contrast to Leopold I; the son was a Belgian Prince, the father a cos-
mopolitan. The latter corresponded with Thiers,
Guizot, Metternich, the Archduke John, his dearly beloved niece, Victoria, and the Coburgs of Portugal and
Germany: this interchange of letters was characteristic
of the period when rulers formed one vast European
family, a society of kings. Leopold II also carried on
a correspondence, but hardly ever with kings, and, in
any case, very infrequently with members of his family.
Leopold I, a Lutheran, romantic and yet reserved, a
man of the world in his younger days, later a misanthrope, married the most charming woman in France,
yet continued to be incurably homesick for Claremont
in England. Leopold II yearned only for power, was
a bad husband, a stern and unjust father, a bitter and
unhappy man, absorbed in his own ambitions and great
projects.

The death-bed of Leopold I was a sad one, with something puritanical and cold about it. In his death agony,
he called: "Charlotte . . . Charlotte . . ." but no one

knew whether he were calling to his daughter, the Empress of Mexico, or to that first Charlotte of Claremont and those enchanted years whose happy memories once more unfolded before his darkening eyes.

"Do you regret the sins you have committed, Sire?" asked his daughter-in-law. He sighed heavily, and answered: "Yes. . . ."

"In the name of the love you bear for the Queen's memory," went on the wife of Leopold II, "will you not be converted to her religion so that you may meet her again in Heaven?"

"Nein . . ." he whispered.

Thus died the first King of the Belgians.

A hundred years after Leopold I's accession to the throne, his grandson, Albert I, explained: "My grandfather was forty-one when he became King. His early triumphs, as well as his tastes, bound him to an era that had passed. He married again late in life, and there was naturally a great difference of age in the first place, and of mentality in the second, between him and his son, my uncle Leopold II. I myself was so much younger than my own father that unfortunately the gap between us was far greater than is normal between parents and children."

At the time of his accession, Leopold II was thirty. Albert I was thirty-five when he became King, and Leopold III was thirty-two. Of the English Saxe-Coburgs, the Prince of Wales did not become King until he was middle-aged. In Belgium, the heir to the throne has no time to grow old; and in a hundred years, Belgium has been fortunate enough to have had three young kings.

Brought up by a very devout mother, Leopold II was "an inconsistent Catholic . . . but a practising Catholic and a firm believer," according to M. Woeste. He spoke with a nasal accent, had a prominent nose, a fan-shaped beard, had suffered from his eighth year from a slight and mysterious lameness, had a passion for work and travel, loved building and scorned popularity. He was an abnormal and extraordinary figure, simultaneously loathed and respected, who contrived to give his incredulous country an empire eighty times larger than itself.

When he returned from Turkey at the age of twenty-two, he had brought back a piece of marble from the Acropolis, and had had engraved upon it: "Belgium must have a colony. . . ." In his speeches to the Senate, where he had been privileged to sit since he had reached his majority, he spoke of opening new trade-routes in Egypt and the Far East. His projects struck a very new or a very old note, such as his plan to explore the ancient Zaire of the Portuguese, that river we now call the Congo, and whose course in the heart of unknown territory in the Black Continent was but dimly guessed. When Stanley returned from his first voyage of discovery across Africa, Victorian England listened to him and shook its head. Whereupon Leopold II instantly sent for the famous journalist, and pressed him into his own service. England had no love for great adventurers; Leopold II adored them because he was an adventurer himself.

However, he never saw the Congo with his own eyes; he preferred to stay at home with his maps and charts,

like the Portuguese Kings in the days of their glory. "I will never let the negroes see a lame king," he would say, in the same way as he once said: "My grandfather, Louis-Philippe, loved to show himself on the balcony. . . . I do not. . . ."

Nevertheless, this did not prevent him from enjoying himself in Paris or Deauville.

The Belgians thought he was a very great man, but too aloof from them; even though the Zaire was soon to become Belgian Congo, people believed that it was too good to be true, like those other fantastic political structures the King had dreamed of setting up in China, Ethiopia and the Soudan. Parliamentary countries do not like projects that are entirely conceived in the mind of one man.

CHAPTER II

CHILDHOOD, YOUTH, AND MARRIAGE

THE Count and Countess of Flanders, brother and sister-in-law of Leopold II, led a devoted and untroubled life together—an uneventful and uninspired existence. From his grandfather, Louis-Philippe, Count Philippe had inherited courage and intelligence, to say nothing of thrift. Not content with making good investments, he rejoiced in petty economies; and he experienced a thoroughly French satisfaction in effecting any small saving—the satisfaction one might feel, for example, in evading some slight task.

The Countess of Flanders cherished the memory of her sister who had married King Pedro of Portugal in 1858, and had died fifteen months later. Three of her brothers were also dead. Antoine of Hohenzollern had been killed at Königgrätz in 1866. Leopold, who died in 1902, had been an unsuccessful candidate for the Spanish throne in 1870, and this rivalry for the crown around which so much intrigue had centred, had been one of the causes of the Franco-Prussian War. Only one of the brothers had survived. This was Charles, who had left Weinburg with a Swiss passport on which his name was given as Karl Weinburg. This passport took him to Roumania, where he became King.

It was said that in 1870 the Countess had done her utmost to dissuade her brother Leopold from accepting

the crown of Spain. It was also said that Baron Noth-
omb, the Belgian Ambassador in Berlin, had been in-
strumental in arranging her betrothal to his great friend,
the Count of Flanders. In any event, it was in Berlin
that this marriage was consecrated in 1867, in the
Church of St. Hedwig, by the Prince-Bishop of Breslau.
The enthusiasm it aroused in Germany caused offence
in the Tuileries where, that same year, the young couple
paid a state visit. Their stay came to a sorrowful end
with the news of Queretaro where Maximilian, Emperor of Mexico, was assassinated. Thus, the Count
and Countess of Flanders spent their entire lives in the
midst of triumph and tragedy, although destined themselves for neither one nor the other. Prince Baudouin,
their eldest son, was born on June 4, 1869. November
of the following year saw the birth of Princess Hen-
rietta. Princess Josephine was born on October 18,
1872, and Prince Albert on April 8, 1875.

The Count of Flanders, although he was essentially
good-natured, and not wanting in acumen, fell into the
habit of eternally grumbling and scoffing. He was to
be seen in the streets of Brussels every morning, but
none of the passers-by paid any attention to him. He
never worried about what people might think of him,
since he never had an opportunity of hearing their
opinions. When occasionally during the daily round
a suggestion was made that threatened to interfere with
his plans, he feigned ignorance; and business documents
had to be thrust under his very nose. . . .

Under his dull régime, everything that children did
or wanted to do was taboo. All requests for holidays,

games or amusement invariably met with an uncompromising refusal. Worse still, the desire to work was as rigorously discouraged as the desire to play. The Count, who had become stone-deaf, used to say in a muffled voice: "When I am gone, everything will be finished." What he meant was that after his death there would no longer be a Belgian King nor a Belgian Monarchy, and that his sons, Baudouin as well as Albert, would be wiser to put such costly luxuries out of their heads.

The Countess of Flanders was undoubtedly more broad-minded, intellectual and generous than her husband, though he was absolute master in this austere house. She was left to fill up her spare time with literature, art and good works. Nor did she fail to do so. A devoutly religious woman, as constant in her attendance at lectures as she was at church services, she had a predilection for literary gatherings. She presided at typical Brussels meetings, and it was she who summoned Brunetière, then at the zenith of his fame, and induced him to lecture a dozen times in the course of one winter. Leopold II held her in high esteem, and called her "Our Lady of Flanders." She took lessons in painting, read the *Revue des Deux Mondes,* surrounded herself with women who shared her tastes, and deserved to be regarded as a pattern to her sex.

But in what a state of neglect the mind of her second son was left! Whilst every care was lavished on Baudouin, the first-born, the heir to the throne, Albert was relegated to a corner of the palace. Leopold II never noticed him. After the death of his own son, the great-

est sorrow of his life, the old King had gradually centred all his royal affection on Baudouin, and, soon rec-
ognizing him to be a true descendant of his race, clever,
fascinating and hard-working, had taken him utterly to
his heart. Baudouin was Leopold's heir-presumptive:
Albert had no place in his thoughts. It had already cost
him too great an emotional effort to re-build around
Baudouin the ambitious structure that had collapsed
with the death of his first heir. Baudouin would reign;
Albert must do the best he could. It is questionable
whether his uncle even knew whether he were studying,
and if so, with whom.

We know to-day. Albert I sometimes spoke with a
bitter smile of those years of bored adolescence. His
tutors were M. Godfroid, a high-school master who
became an officer in the mercantile marine, no one
knows quite why, and M. Sigogne. We feel that it was
not on account of his superlative merit as a teacher that
M. Godfroid left his scholastic profession. As for M.
Sigogne, we know that he was Swiss, and held a Chair
at the University of Liége, somewhat pretentiously
styled the Chair of Rhetoric. If rhetoric merely con-
sists in the pronunciation of innumerable words, it is
possible that M. Sigogne was an orator. I have before
me a small volume of essays on contemporary subjects
that emanated from his pen, and was dedicated to Albert I, then Prince Albert. It is difficult to see how such
a collection of balderdash could have been dedicated to
so great a mind. M. Sigogne had ideas on democracy,
the republic, and the rights of man; and he intended

to inculcate them into his royal pupil.   The latter must indeed have had a strong sense of humour to have withstood the battery of so many platitudes, whilst preserving a taste for study.   How he must have laughed, later, when he re-read M. Sigogne's little book.

As the Countess grew older, she devoted herself increasingly to the arts and good works.   Mlle. Hoebrechts, and Jacobs, the violinist, gave command performances of Beethoven, Mozart and Chopin.   She interested herself in the welfare of the people, and awarded prizes in competitions organized to promote hygiene and the erection of model dwellings.   Every afternoon she was to be seen in the park with her dogs, which she called her "Autumn dogs . . . because their coats were as golden as the fallen leaves."

When the Count died, his widow left his personal belongings untouched on his table—his cigar-box, watchcase, pen-knife, and a portrait of Prince Baudouin by Vanaise.

This high standard of morality, howsoever lacking in imagination, made a deep impression in Belgium. Though its effect on youth may have been stifling, its orderliness and conventionality filled the respectable middle-classes with admiration.   What is more, the cavalier fashion with which the domestic virtues were treated at the Olympus of Laeken still further enhanced the popularity of the Rue de la Régence.   At the close of her life, all the grandmothers in Belgium were modelling themselves on the Countess of Flanders.

When Prince Albert had somehow succeeded in getting through his preliminary studies, it was incumbent on him to begin his training as a soldier. He entered the Military School, which then had its headquarters in the white buildings in the Abbey of La Cambre, on the southern side of Brussels. In this valley, near a spring, there were woods: thrushes chirped in gardens at the foot of a hill; there was a stagnant marsh.

During the Middle Ages, all the country around Brussels had been full of refuges for prayer and meditation, from Forest to Bonne-Odeur, from Groenendael to Vauvert. The Abbey of La Cambre, or Canura, had formerly been one of eleven religious houses in the Brabançon Forest. By the time the Belgian Princes were students, however, the original character of this foundation had become no more than a mystic memory, lending force, perhaps, to the austere temper of the School. Here were combined two forms of military training— in effect, a combination of the Polytechnic and St. Cyr. But in both branches of the service at La Cambre (ordinary infantry training and technical training), more value was attached to the science of tactics and mathematics than to other subjects.

One December morning in 1890, when a wintry sun was shining, the 42nd promotion class was called out on parade: a new member was about to join its ranks. King Leopold appeared, leaning on his cane, accompanied by the Count and Countess of Flanders, Prince Baudouin—who had trained in the 36th promotion class —and Prince Albert. The bugles blared, the band broke into the "Brabançonne." Prince Baudouin was in

the green uniform of the Carabiniers, the crack infantry regiment in which he held the rank of captain. As decreed by tradition, he had entered the Grenadiers four years earlier; but in order that no jealousy should be created, a casting vote had been given between the two uniforms. Prince Albert wore the black uniform trimmed with scarlet braid, and the badge—a cassowary —of the cadets.

He was not quite sixteen years old. Tall, too tall for his age, somewhat awkward, apt to forget his rank in bursts of gaiety, accustomed only to military company, it might have been supposed, seeing him beside his handsome and intelligent brother, that these two Princes would lead lives similar to those of their uncles, the sons of Louis-Philippe. Orléans, Namours, Aumale and Joinville had grown up worldly and cultured young officers, before they had commanded armies and navies and had become members of learned societies. Destiny, however, had marked out an entirely different path for the Belgian Princes.

At the beginning of January, 1891, the Military School of La Cambre was shaken by profound emotion. Prince Baudouin was dead. He had contracted pneumonia (complicated, it was thought, by haematuria) while he was in camp at Beverloo. During the three weeks of his illness he had written several letters to his brother officers, and had described his symptoms to them. The Palace officials, however, had been unwise enough not to issue bulletins about his health; hence malicious gossip arose; and it was said that he had been

killed in a duel on account of the bright eyes of a lady of high rank.

Prince Baudouin left behind him the memory of a sensitive, almost hypersensitive young man, who was moody yet ardent. He left but little else: a few letters to friends, a few portraits, a few outlined plans. Prince Baudouin would never be forgotten; but in a few years nothing would be known of him.

The obsequies were deeply moving. The cadets of the Military School escorted the bier to St. Gudule, and were dazzled by the brilliant uniforms of the foreign princes and attachés. When the coffin was borne by grenadiers into the cathedral, the cadets presented arms. At the conclusion of the service, the cortège issued forth, drew level with them, and halted. Leopold II had sent for his cloak. There was a delay of two minutes. During this brief space the cadets gazed, motionless, at the tragic coffin draped with a flag, while the muffled drums sounded a mournful knell. The King put on his cloak and went his way, as remote and inaccessible as Jupiter. He was followed by Prince Albert in the black uniform of the School. As the cortège wended its way back to Laeken, the army realized for the first time that it would some day have a King Albert.

Two outstanding personalities had been chosen as advisers to the Prince. Although there were no points of resemblance between them, both Major Jungbluth and Major de Grunne were remarkable men. The former, who had been appointed tutor, exerted the strongest, and very soon the sole, influence during these years.

For a decade the future King was never to be seen except in the company of Jungbluth.

The Prince did not live at the School. He struck people as being somewhat handicapped by his height and his awkward, too youthful, appearance. All his companions in the promotion class were above the legal age of seventeen. He himself was not yet sixteen. They were all extremely proud of their small store of learning, but he, because of his finer brain, was aware of his own ignorance, and suffered in consequence.

Unused as he was to the atmosphere of student-life, he had been abruptly flung into the midst of the rough and tumble. He had been taught by professors who spoke like dictionaries; and with no transition he now found himself surrounded by quick-witted cadets who spoke slang. At this time, the general level of the lectures was very high. Albert instantly realized the gaps in his own knowledge, and, thin-skinned and proud, like all sensitive children who have been neglected, he imagined that people were making fun of him. To make matters worse, cadets were selected to be his companions during the exercise in the courtyard at recess. Companionship was everlastingly imposed on him, friendships were forced on him.

I have scanned the contemporary list of cadets for names that were to make history. Seldom had the School numbered such a brilliant galaxy of pupils. There was Octave Neuray, later a master at La Cambre, now a general. Then I found Cadet Galet, who rose to be Chief of Staff; Cadet Pouleur, who later commanded an army-corps; Cadet Theunis, who became a

colonel in the artillery, and afterward Prime Minister. It was a generation of handsome and virile young men, wholeheartedly devoted to their Prince, but forced to admit to themselves that Albert was backward, had a timid manner, and was not much of a conversationalist.

He himself suffered intensely at La Cambre. "My parents made a great mistake when they sent me there," he often told his friends in later years. "I had had no preparation for that kind of life. The studies, the atmosphere and the talk were entirely strange to me."

The tall stripling, who only saw his father in the evening, whose first masters were semi-educated, whose only refuge was escape, whose sole rewards were impositions, was racked by the sense of his own incompetence and by the agonizing feeling that he was different from others. Meanwhile the Count of Flanders, who was an enthusiastic book-lover, collected rare editions; and his son, watching the shelves fill up with sets in exquisite bindings, wondered if he would ever find the key to that enchanted world.

This existence continued for two years. Every morning the Prince drove to the gates of the School. Every evening the carriage with two footmen in cream-coloured livery came again to fetch him. He went punctiliously through the ritual of drill, class-work, riding and recreation. At the far end of the hall, Jungbluth (whom he called Juth) followed the lectures, and sometimes made notes. When the Prince chanced to see him scribbling, he thought: "Juth is doing my work—I can rest." This was the only breach in the regulations he allowed himself during those two years. When the

final drill was over, Juth reappeared at the other side of the courtyard, invariably in green with golden epaulettes, as lean, as smart, as stiff as ever. At the signal, he took out his watch and looked at the Prince who instantly obeyed, ran eagerly to join him, and fell into step at his side. The instructor was a Captain Schmidt of the Grenadiers, tall, good-looking and fairly competent. During drill, when someone giggled in the ranks, the Captain, in order to show that he made no exceptions, would say: "You again, Your Highness!" which was perfectly inaccurate, as everyone was aware.

During Albert's second year an addition to the staff caused a sensation. This new officer, who had to maintain order and discipline, and take drill, was next in command to the lecturers. The newcomer was Lieutenant Emile Franqui. He was a square-shouldered Walloon of medium height, with a resonant bass voice, who made a far deeper impression by his overwhelming self-confidence than by his knowledge of his work. He had risen from the ranks of the infantry, had very soon taken a dislike to garrison life, and had been one of the first to sail for the Congo. He was known to have been made much of by Leopold II; and the attitude of his colleagues towards him was one of uneasy admiration. At any day, he might go back to Africa, for he was free from all ambition for a military career, and had obviously resolved to serve his King in other directions than the beaten track.

Did the future Ruler guess that for forty-three years the ever-enlarging silhouette of this man would cross his path, and that Franqui would one day become one

of the most prominent figures in international finance
as well as one of the most formidable political influences
in Belgium? All were conscious of his latent power.
He was very dark, had large eyes that sparkled with intelligence, had been in command of negroes for many
years—and of course his pupils nicknamed him Bamboula.

Often, whilst strolling through the gardens of La
Cambre, which has again become a house of the Religious, I have tried to evoke the vanished shadows of
the Military School, now quartered elsewhere. Part of
the old cloister has been restored, and the parade-
ground has been turned into terraced gardens which
reach as far as the Avenue Louise. Thrushes nest there
in the spring, and the drums are heard no more. Yet
the life of the convent resembles that of the Military
School with its rigid time-table, processions, ritual,
childish pleasures, and early rising—for Matins now, not
gymnastics. La Cambre has become a parish church;
but on summer evenings, standing near the entrance to
the courtyard, I have sometimes imagined I could see a
carriage draw up, with Jungbluth's eagle beak at the
door. The Prince crosses the courtyard with huge
strides. Cadets Theunis, Du Bois, Galet, Pouleur,
Fastrets and Neuray jot down notes and figures; and
dominating them all with an air of superior calm, Lieutenant Franqui dreams of Katanga, India and China
. . . there, in the home of the mystic daughters of St.
Bernard.

When he left the School the Prince was gazetted second lieutenant in the Grenadiers, and took the place

in the regiment left empty by his brother. To celebrate, he gave a dinner to his friends in the Rue Fossé aux Loups. Everyone except Albert was in the highest spirits.

At this time it seemed as though no one but Jungbluth could influence the Prince. There was, of course, Major de Grunne; but between these two officers there could be no question of shared interests—there could only be competition. But for the uniform they wore, they were in entire contrast to one another. Major Jungbluth was enigmatic and austere, and his brilliant brain had absorbed far more than mere classical knowledge. He was sufficiently high-minded to think only of his pupil, yet distrustful enough to ward off any possible rival and to be on the alert for the slightest signs of ascendency in any but himself. No one could accuse him of opportunism, since he had been devoted to the Prince long before Albert had become heir to the throne. Jungbluth, though too discerning to keep the Prince from the society of those from whom he might derive benefit, was sensitive enough to take exception to whatever influence, however slight, they might exert on him.

He encouraged a taste for general knowledge in the Prince, laying no particular stress on Greek or Latin. When the Jesuit Father Castelein was asked to give Albert lessons in philosophy and ethics, he found that he possessed an extraordinarily retentive memory but that he had practically no knowledge of literature. It may be said of Jungbluth that he did not introduce a single

injurious idea or a single bad friend to the Prince. But he too often avoided introducing good ones.

In contrast to Jungbluth, Count François de Henricourt de Grunne stood for tradition, chivalry and eloquence. He was an ardent Catholic, the son-in-law of Montalembert; an aristocrat to his finger-tips. As such, he was attractive even in his inhibitions and conventions. He came to the Machine Age spiritually clad in the armour of the thirteenth century, with the heart and mind of a Crusader. His nature had inclined him more towards the history of warfare than towards its practice, and he had soon become a lecturer at the Ecole de Guerre where he taught brilliantly, his words ringing out in passionate vindication of the glories of bygone ages. Incapable of scheming, he was equally incapable of unmasking the intrigues of others.

Such an idealist was bound to be constantly sacrificed. He was generous and eager, gay and romantic. Jungbluth was unemotional and austere, competent and laconic. Major de Grunne's nature urged him to transform the Prince into an instrument of Divine Right, whilst Major Jungbluth sought to make a modern Telemachus of him, moulded from the clay of democracy, on the principles of the Social Contract. Above all, Jungbluth clung tenaciously to his position, determined not to be dislodged; de Grunne dreamed of education, and was ready, should the signal be given, to resume his Chair of History. This soon came about; and Major de Grunne, with no sense of bitterness—he was utterly incapable of any such feeling, apparently— left the field to his victorious rival.

It might have been better had he been able to remain in the Palace of Flanders. An optimist, like all saints of his type, he would have diffused a little sweetness where there was later to be so much gall and wormwood. Perhaps his wholly chivalrous nature would not have sufficed for the education of a twentieth century prince, but it would have brought him happiness; and Jungbluth, despite his many qualifications, had not this gift to confer.

The Palace of Flanders stands near the Place Royale. A few yards away, Lower Brussels swarms with life and movement. This is the *quartier* of La Chapelle and the Marolles. Ever since the fifteenth century, the voice of the people has risen thence—soft or scolding, loving or critical. Here the weavers and fullers of the Middle Ages held their meetings and drew up their charters; here were the lazar-houses, ghettos and workshops; here were innumerable alleys that had no outlet, crowded with an incredible confusion of hawkers peddling their wares. Far below the gleaming wealth of church-spires, far below the monuments, a scene teeming with life could be perceived.

Close to the public thoroughfare and the Palace is the Library, that incomparable treasure inherited from the Grand Dukes of the West, from Charles V, and the Hapsburgs at the pinnacle of their glory. A little higher up is the Royal Palace, its gardens, and the square where the troops parade. In the centre of the Place Royale stands a picturesque statue of Godefroid de Bouillon. Thus, during those early years, the Prince

lived midway between Upper and Lower Brussels, between Leopold II and the Maison du Peuple, between
his beloved Library and the statue of the famous Duke
of Lothier.

But the carriages that drew up in the tiny courtyard
of the Palace of Flanders brought only charming and
courteous guests from the world of society, never Socialists or revolutionaries from Lower Brussels. I wonder
if, by the preference he openly showed in later years for
his Socialist subjects, the King were avenging himself in
some obscure way for the boring years of his youth?

I have often imagined a dialogue between the Church
of La Chapelle down below, and the Church of St.
Jacques above. "I have existed for nine hundred years,"
says La Chapelle, "and my walls hold as many legends,
stories, prayers and memories as an entire province.
The poor have crowded their dwellings round me—
those same poor who had no vote in the nineteenth century, spoke in rude dialect, lived in hovels, and wore
bonnets and sabots. The worthy gentlemen of St.
Vincent de Paul occasionally saw fit to visit them and
me. But all who came from this neighbourhood, the
neighbourhood of vagrants and beggars, were of necessity mad and dangerous—so thought the bourgeoisie.
But the King spent his youth quite close to us. He listened to us, and understood. . . ."

And St. Jacques replies: "I, with my clock, whose
hands are always at a standstill, was built during the
reign of Maria-Theresa, the era of the decadent bourgeoisie. Despite myself, I gave asylum to a European
King and an Adventurer King. I have seen the baptism

of Leopold II, Albert I, and Leopold III. My entire
domain is royal, almost too royal for my poor walls; the
chestnut trees of the Palace gardens grow as high as my
roof. La Chapelle is older than I, it is true, but nearer
to the gutter, the kingdom of beer, and the vendors of
snails. I am the great church, full of memories of the
kings of distant lands, of voyages across the sea, and of
great European conflicts. . . ."

And St. Jacques, like La Chapelle, is right. Yet if a
King sought to win over La Chapelle, it seemed that he
must inevitably alienate or scandalize St. Jacques. The
great art of Albert's reign was to lie in imparting wisdom to both, in reconciling the two. But in 1895 the
Countess of Flanders was devoting herself body and
soul to good works, and the Count of Flanders was utterly engrossed in his collection of rare books.

When the Belgian people were told that the Prince
divided his time between study, travel, and the command of a company of Grenadiers, they smiled, hesitated, and concluded by saying: "Well, perhaps it's
true. . . ." So many princes had plunged into the life
of pleasure, scarcely troubling to conceal their light
amours, that the man in the street found it hard to believe in the idea of a serious-minded young Prince who
hoped to marry the woman of his choice, and who refused to take a hand in politics.

Prince Albert made few friendships, but studied
much, went down into the mines, visited factories incognito, took the salute at all important reviews, and
still found time to follow his career as an officer. In

spite of what has been said to the contrary, he thoroughly enjoyed the time he spent in camp at Beverloo. He did his share of the work, and even checked the regimental accounts.

It was an age of industrialism, and the country was overflowing with wealth and work. The Prince was always more inclined towards political economy than strategy; and the system of trusts, syndicates, co-operative societies and companies made so great an appeal to his alert mind that his interest was immediately aroused. Here, too, Jungbluth's education bore fruit. Albert's secretary was a little Fleming from Limbourg, a mere youth, who was taking a course of political economy at Louvain. The Prince would ask his secretary for his note-books, and the two would pursue the subject together. M. Jules Ingenbleek was a typical Belgian, with a fund of common sense and energy—exactly the kind of man for whom the Prince was looking. Albert was as interested in the student as the study, and seemed to hear through him the voice of the Flemish country— that voice unknown in official Brussels, except as interpreted by land-owners and priests.

Princely tradition prescribed a visit to the United States; and thither Albert went, accompanied by Jungbluth, in 1898. Ever since the time of M. de Toqueville, it had been expected of a serious-minded Prince that he would cross the Atlantic, visit Philadelphia, and study at first hand the working-out of Jefferson's enlightened dreams. It was equally part of the tradition that he should receive proposals of marriage from the heiresses of the New World; and Albert did receive them

by the score. Jungbluth kept the list. Not even Boni de Castellane himself was so sought after as Albert I at the same age. In these matters, too, Jungbluth played the part of mentor, and, duly authorized by Leopold II, kept the boldest suitors at bay. Several families had taken care to put their proposals in writing, so that the substantial nature of their offers should be known at Laeken. At the close of his life, Jungbluth enjoyed telling the story of this journey of his Telemachus.

Plans were being made for Albert's marriage, and the people, ignorant of his own intentions, also discussed possible matches for him. Leopold II had made rigorous stipulations, and had drawn up a black list and a white list—the black list, needless to say, being very much longer than the white. It almost seemed as though the old King, who was crowding more and more amorous adventures into his last years, were seeking to prevent youth from contracting a happy marriage because he himself had been denied that experience. This was the period when Princess Clémentine, having fallen in love with Prince Victor Napoleon, was strictly guarded by the police in order that no such abomination as a union with a Buonaparte should become a *fait accompli*. Jungbluth had received instructions of the same sort. The Prince was young, attractive, and very tall. Jungbluth was short, with a Jewish profile, but slender and erect—it was he who kept both lists concealed beneath his green cloak.

In the end, however, the Prince chose his own bride. She was the daughter of Prince Charles Theodor, a Bavarian duke, a descendant of the illustrious House

of Wittelsbach.   Leopold II could raise no objection, and the statesmen could not interfere.   Albert's life, in which gaiety, pleasure and love had hitherto had no part, was now crowned by real romance, and the idyll pursued its happy course to the sound of music, in a setting of edelweiss.

Portraits of the youthful lovers are rare.   However, I have come across a signed photograph in the possession of a private family.   The Prince looks very slim and disconcertingly elegant in frock-coat, black tie, and with a pointed beard which gives him the appearance of a young artist.   The Princess, who already faithfully fore-shadowed the woman she was to become, has the same stately and fluid grace; she looks dignified notwithstand-ing her tiny stature.   Both are earnest, distinguished, and obviously in love.   Their signatures are symbolic. His is deliberate and careful.   Hers is in bold characters, and the capital letters are brave flourishes.   His is the hand of a scholar, hers the penmanship of a queen.

M. Gustave Van Zype, a contemporary journalist, managed to insinuate himself into the intimate circle at Possenhoven.   At the betrothal festivities, he saw the charming white house where Prince Charles Theodor enjoyed the peace that springs from a harmonious home life and a successful career.   He was a brilliant oculist, and his happiest days were spent in the Munich hos-pitals where he gave free treatment.   His was an en-lightened mind: he was said to be tainted by Voltairian-ism, even though his wife was the Princess of Orléans-Braganza.   His three daughters (one of whom married Rupprecht of Bavaria, while the youngest became the

wife of Count Törring) were in every way worthy of him. Princess Elisabeth adored music and science, was a splendid horsewoman, and had been carefully educated.

The betrothal festivities were such as might have been expected in a castle, with two royal lovers as the central figures of the romance. The officers of the Palace had followed their Prince to Possenhoven. "Don't disturb the children," said Duke Charles Theodor; "leave them alone, and we will go for a ride." He himself rode extremely well, but too hard and in relays; that is to say, after an hour he would call for a fresh mount in the heart of the country and gallop off again. Jungbluth soon found this form of exercise too taxing.

The festivities, concerts, charity functions, rides, the simplicity, the rural life—all this charmed the Belgian people and the young couple themselves. The Brussels public eagerly read M. Van Zype's outpourings in the *Gazette:*

"On the stroke of five, the military band in the next room struck up a waltz; the door of the Charlemagne salon opened, and the procession entered. At its head was the slight figure of Princess Elisabeth, walking with slow steps. She wore a white satin dress cut just low enough to show her smooth delicately-shaped shoulders and the graceful column of her throat. A simple coronet circled her chestnut curls. There was a burning blush on her cheek—she was obviously moved. The Prince's face matched the crimson ribbon on his breast. They talked to each other as they moved along; the

Princess, who looked even lovelier than on the previous night, gazed up at her tall cavalier.

"When they had taken their seats, she had eyes for no one but the Prince who was on her left. She took no heed of the King of Roumania on her other side, the Regent who was seated a little further away, nor of the score or so of princes and princesses who were present. The tiny pages shyly offered the dishes that were handed to them by the footmen. I noticed that the young Princess scarcely took anything; she ate nothing, but talked incessantly to Prince Albert who would nervously crumble his bread whenever the King of Roumania claimed his fiancée's attention for a minute. The two seemed to be absorbed in a world of their own. No one could see them without realizing that this Prince and Princess were true lovers, and that this was their hour; the throne, the historic past evoked by the setting, their exalted rank, their dazzling surroundings might have been non-existent. Their only thoughts were for each other, for their future life together. Their love shed such a lustre over them that everything paled beside them, or, rather, was transfigured, gaining in nobility what was lost in brilliance. They were in love, and at that moment, they were only a man and a maid. The guests themselves were metamorphosed. No longer were they kings, duchesses, generals, ladies-in-waiting— the human touch had made them oblivious of their rank, and in the presence of the lovers, they had become simple men and women. The lights streamed down on radiant faces, on shoulders that would have been as lovely without the glitter of necklaces, eyes that would

have sparkled as brilliantly without the answering flash
of coronets. . . ."

The royal pair came to live in Brussels, and chose a
house in the Rue de la Science which runs parallel to
the Rue de l'Industrie. There a son was born to them
in 1901, a second in 1903, and a daughter in 1906. Leopold, Charles and Marie-José—three traditional Belgian
names, three flaxen heads, three alert little minds. All
that was known of the royal household was that its in-
mates were devotedly attached to each other: their private life was their own.

At the beginning of 1909 the Prince visited the
Congo. After long and labyrinthine discussions, King
Leopold had at last relaxed his hold on the territory of
his commercial conquest and had given it in trust to
his country. It behoved the future King to visit the
new territory which the Dynasty would bequeath him.
Accompanied by an aide-de-camp and a Colonial
official, he landed at the Cape and for the first time set
foot in that Continent of Africa where he had so often
wandered in imagination. The Prince walked, rode
and cycled, from the gold-mines of Johannesburg to the
falls of the Congo, from the delightful country of the
Cape to the sweltering wastes of Kasai, from the high
plateaux of Katanga to the burning rocks of the lower
Congo—some five thousand miles. By this time, he
had acquired all that his position exacted of him: a
wide knowledge of economic problems, a solid grasp of
the conditions necessary for a colonial venture, and the
judgment which results from years of travel, study and

meditation. He travelled by way of the Vaal and Rhodesia from south to north, to the very heart of the dark continent.

Those who knew him at this period were struck by his gaiety, his unaffected manners, and the keen interest he displayed in everything. He was at the height of his physical vigour; although he enjoyed a glass of wine with his meals, he was a moderate drinker, and he took so little interest in food that he was quite content with dry biscuits when nothing else was available. At night, when mosquitoes swarmed round the flares which cast their flickering light on faces, maps and papers, he buried himself in books of travel and English essays.

Gradually, during the long stages by wagon, the slow progress along the sluggish grey rivers while the rowers chanted monotonously, his whole view of the world began to change. It must have been there that he strengthened his natural bent for invariably consulting his map—for searching out the spot where an event had occurred. When he spoke of the Congo towards the end of his reign, it often struck me that he had acquired his immense store of geographical-historical knowledge on his expeditions through the Bush.

The Katanga was causing him anxiety at that time, because this most southerly portion of the Empire ad-joined Rhodesia and was most exposed to British covet-ousness. Everything, as he now saw, depended on link-ing these high plateaux, where it was so cold at night that the fires paled and died out, to the torrid shores of the Atlantic. In Katanga, the land of radium, the Prince worked out averages in horse-power and mileage,

and made calculations in kilometres. (During this sort of mental exercise, his hands would wander absently over the globe.) The habit grew on him to such an extent that, towards the end of his life, he would pick up railway time-tables and work out speed averages to the hundreth part of a kilometre, for sheer distraction.

I am not sure whether he was shown all that he wanted to see during that first voyage. Incidentally, he was wise enough not to have formed his opinions beforehand. During one of his journeys a party of Englishmen lured away his bearers, who had pledged their word to remain with him. This enabled him to measure the fickleness of the black brain, and the worth of palavers between employers and employés in the land of ebony. The British press was full of bitter denunciations of Leopold's policy. Albert was able to assure himself that the Transvaalians were equally hard on the Kaffirs and Zulus, and the Germans on the Herreros.

By an unfortunate coincidence, that year, 1909, was the worst in the history of the anti-Leopoldian polemic. Morel continued to publish his famous anathemas in the *Review of Reviews,* and through the medium of the Congo Reform Association; what was even more serious, the Archbishop of Canterbury presided at a mass meeting in the Albert Hall, and added his powerful voice to the accusing chorus. The Alexander motion against the Belgian Congo was voted at a meeting of the Peace League; and Conan Doyle brought out his book: *The Crime of the Congo.* Meanwhile, the *Times* advocated "an attitude of close vigilance" and provoked the angry protests of the Congo Reformers. Conan Doyle

wrote a letter to the great newspaper, in which he said:
"I have read the article on the Congo question in your
columns with deep regret."

In order to weigh the pros and cons of the problem,
it was just as well that Albert himself should have visited
Africa. In addition to his observations of the conditions of life and the economic situation of the Congo,
he brought back from his journey a collection of care-
fully-sifted scientific facts; and his first gift on the day
after his coronation was a sum of five hundred pounds
to the School of Medicine at Liverpool, to be devoted to
the campaign against sleeping-sickness.

On July 18, 1909, when he reached the Atlantic port
of Boma, a German cruiser, which was lying out in the
bay, fired a salvo of guns in his honour. This cruiser
was the *Panther*. There it lay beneath a burning sun;
and at night its lights swayed gently under the Southern
Cross as if to warn the King-to-be that after Katanga
and the Bush there would be Agadir, Serajevo and the
Yser.

Four months later, Leopold II died.

To-day in Belgium, you often hear it said: "That's
well-built—it must belong to the period of Leopold
II," or else: "What a well-chosen site—Leopold II must
have picked it out." So, in 1909, people in Brussels
said with the same sense of conviction: "That's one of
the old King's idiotic notions. . . . When Albert becomes king, everything will be different."

When Leopold II died the Belgians displayed more

astonishment than admiration for the wonders he had accomplished. In his Palace at Laeken, three miles from Brussels, he had lived amidst palms and orchids, remote from the people. He had reigned so long that he seemed to have thrown down a challenge to time. Of his children only Princess Clémentine remained with him. His whole life long, the old King had sown the seeds of scandal and bitterness. His parsimony had become a byword, and all sorts of stories were told about his miserliness, down to the very wages he paid his gardeners. In 1876 the priests had cut *Domine salvum fac regem* from the prayer which follows the Mass. English and American clergy had instituted pious crusades against the Congo, spreading accounts of mutilated and crucified blacks. Anseele, the Socialist deputy of Ghent, had denounced the King as a murderer. The upper middle-classes had looked down on him with the self-sufficient pride of those who feel that they have been slighted.

Yet the close of Leopold II's reign was marked by two great triumphs. First, the Congo had become a Belgian Colony in October, 1908, and on November 15 the tri-coloured flag of Brabant had been substituted for the notorious blue standard spangled with golden stars that until then had waved under the tropical sun. The Belgian people had accepted the gift without enthusiasm, but Cardinal Mercier had had a *Te Deum* sung in thanksgiving on November 1, All Saints' Day. Secondly, the law concerning military service which the King had made so many attempts to establish, had at last been passed in the Chamber; and

on his death-bed, Leopold could sign the decree which would give Belgium the beginning of the standing army of which she stood in increasing need.

On the evening of December 1, 1909, he came back to Brussels from Paris by the eleven o'clock train, very tired, hardly recognizable. On Sunday, December 12, he said to his valet: "This is the end." He sent for the priest from Laeken, and asked for the Last Sacraments.

On the fourteenth, he said to the priest: "I was anxious to see you again to-night. I wanted you to be near me. I tried to say a prayer, but I could not remember my *Pater*. . . ."

All Brussels was aware that he was living with his mistress. She was known as Baroness Vaughan, was handsome in a coarse way, and was a woman of the people. She had borne him two children; and when she was ordered to leave the Palace, her position was found to have been regularized: the King had gone through a religious ceremony with her.

The last confession of Leopold II was worthy of Louis XIV. In a loud voice, he said: "What you are asking me to do is hard indeed. But God is the Mighty Sovereign—His will be done."

On the night of his death, he murmured: "His Majesty is thirsty. . . ." This was on December 17. At half past two in the morning, he had breathed his last. Disorderly crowds thronged the streets of Brussels, sowing scabrous pamphlets broadcast. Those who were sincerely moved dared not show their emotion.

Albert was sent for at once: he was King.

CHAPTER III

THE KING AND HIS PEOPLE

AS a rule, when a very old king dies, his successor feels it incumbent upon him to impress the people by some outstanding triumph of contrast. Albert I was able to create an immediate impression merely by going on with his normal way of life. He was thirty-four, the happy father of a united family. He was very hard-working and a smart officer, although somewhat handicapped by shyness and a slight awkwardness when he came before the public eye. It was known that he was extremely well-read; that he had travelled a great deal; and that the young Queen was clever, lively and perceptive.

There had not been a queen in Belgium for many years, and the people were delighted to welcome one again. Unconsciously, she became the symbol of a new order—a new morality that was a mixture of earnestness and gaiety. This was the atmosphere of life at Laeken under Albert and Elisabeth.

It was a Court full of life and energy; when they were in the country, the Queen would go riding at seven in the morning. It was an erudite Court; the King frequently invited Professor Waxweiler of the Solvay Institute to lunch, and discussed sociology with him from the soup to the savoury. It was a Court that was continually changing its venue; the King loved travelling—

always with the Queen, whom he invariably referred to as "my wife." It was a philanthropic and imaginative Court, passionately addicted to mountaineering and colonial studies, aviation, natural science, botany, medicine, literature and Judaism.

No sovereign of modern times has been so badly dressed. Except when he had to wear uniform, the King gave no thought to his appearance. Portraits taken of him at the beginning of his reign do show a certain care in the fit of his clothes and the cutting of his hair. But as he grew older, he bade good-bye to tailors, hairdressers and manicurists. The people of Brussels used to say: "The King walks about with the money for his barber in his pocket." At heart, though, they were pleased by this royal indifference, this absence of formality in externals. (On the tragic night of his death, I was admitted into his bedroom and passed through his dressing-room. Never again shall I set eyes on such a wardrobe. On circular stands, weird coats of no style or period were hanging, topped off with those singular hats, of the sort worn by entomologists or planters, which he bought in Switzerland and used both in the Congo and the Bernese Oberland.)

In his first Speech from the Throne, the new King had spoken at great length of the vital reforms to be made in the social legislation of the Congo. As usual, the man in the street distorted facts: Leopold II became an Old Man of the Mountain, Albert I a president who, at the conclusion of the banquet, accepts a crown with loud shouts of: "Long live the Republic!" As usual, too, the onlooker saw only one side of things,

and believed that the King's informal appearance and friendly manner betrayed a bourgeois streak in him. Yet no one in Belgium could have been less bourgeois than he. Were I seeking a word to describe both the King and Queen, I should choose the word *bohemian,* the exact opposite of bourgeois. Yes, bohemian, notwithstanding their devout sense of duty, their happy marriage, their firm insistence on order in the house, in the country, and in literature. They were bohemian in their unprejudiced outlook, their lack of snobbishness, their love of adventure, their indifference to danger, etiquette, and criticism. They were in nowise bound within the conventional limits of the bourgeois conception of life—life as lived by men of property, great or small, in the twentieth century. Real kings, those with kingship in their blood, have always loved the working-classes, Jews, scholars, inventors and heroes.

The only flaw in this régime was that those who, in the ordinary way, would have been the principal habitués of the Court—the noble families, officials, merchants, princes, diplomats—were kept at a distance. These never met the King except at the annual Court Ball and the exclusive reception on New Year's Day. The aristocratic quarter of Brussels was that least visited by the King.

Let us picture Albert and Elisabeth in the privacy of their grounds. The King is seated at the wheel of his little car; the Queen has brought a friend with her—perhaps Claus, the artist, or Rousseau, the sculptor, or Emile Verhaeren, the poet, or Dr. Nolf, the family physician. The royal driver "steps on it"—he is happy

—these friends of his do not attend the genteel drawing-rooms where he himself never goes, and they will not give him away. . . .

It is small wonder that the King sought refuge, as often as might be, in the easy bohemianism of his intimate circle. His political heritage from the days of Leopold II was not an easy one. The Congo affair had already passed its critical phase, to be sure. But, in the few years between his accession and the very eve of the War, Albert had to deal by slow constitutional means with two major problems at home—with the crises of two great popular movements. The first of these, Belgian Socialism, was at bottom a matter of economic geography. The second, Flemish Nationalism, although it sprang from the same roots as the other, was largely a sentimental issue. It was none the less dangerous, naturally, on that account.

If we look on the map of Belgium for the Republican or Socialist zone, we shall find first a northern boundary which extends from Visé to Tournai, and a southern boundary which runs from Seraing to Philippeville. Between them is the Red country, shrouded in smoke from factory-chimneys, where the blood of men is so hot that any trifle may cause a strike. This is the Walloon country where the people are all for France and the tri-colour. Jacobin and anti-clerical, they love to hold forth, and work themselves up to a fever with mechanically-rendered "Marseillaises." The worker has suffered long and bitterly. He is not lacking in dignity, the will to work, or honesty. For forty years, he has

been deeply influenced by Marxist ideas, so deeply that the co-operative movement and proletarian organization have developed to an amazing extent. Nowhere, with the possible exception of Denmark, is so complete a Socialist world to be found.

When Albert I came to the throne the Walloon country was, as it still is, entirely Republican. The King went there freely, however, and was greeted without any resentment or anti-monarchic demonstrations. It was an extraordinary contradiction in terms that, *per se*, the Red Deputy was both Communist and Loyalist. A few deputies were actually affiliated to the Internationale; yet they were ardent patriots. Thus, the Socialist Syndicate would shout: "Long live the Republic!" within the closed doors of the Maison du Peuple, and "Long live the King!" in the streets. Attracted by this unexpected duality, the liberal bourgeoisie practised something of the same sort. They resembled those Parisians of the Left Wing who adore the visits of foreign royalties, and, although they have crowned Labour, cheer royal processions to the echo.

To the south of this zone lie the Ardennes, full of traditions, famed for agriculture, trade and forestry. The majority of writers, priests and captains of industry come from this part of Belgium. To the north of Wallonia, however, we enter the Flemish country. Here we find Socialism with a difference—and also with a longer history.

In the year 1880, there lived in Ghent a workman by the name of Edouard Anseele, who was obsessed by the

desire to make this world a better place. He was the
son of a shoemaker who had a small shop in the Rue
Longue des Penitentes, close to the Church of St.
Jacques. This is the most populous corner of ancient
Ghent, and is near the Marché du Vendredi. The
elder Anseele lived, therefore, in a semi-revolutionary,
semi-ecclesiastical setting, where the church clock
chimed the hours but where no one dreamed of attacking the Hôtel de Ville, which was entirely in the
hands of the bourgeoisie.

In his earlier years, young Anseele was educated by
the Brethren of the Christian Schools, and was forced
by necessity to earn his daily bread. But when the
neighbouring College, which was state-owned, caught
fire, Edouard Anseele rendered such energetic aid in
fighting the flames that, by way of thanks, he was allowed to complete his studies there without payment.
After leaving, he obtained employment, subsequently
went to America with eighty francs in his pocket, soon
wearied of the life, and returned to Belgium, where he
obtained a post in the firm of Fievez.

Later on, he became a printer and a revolutionary.
In his leisure hours, he translated the works of Zola
into Flemish. Copies of *Germinal,* translated by
Edouard Anseele, are still to be found in the second-
hand bookshops of Ghent. He had a gift for eloquence;
he harangued the people in a husky voice, and his language, full of imagery, was a mixture of the vernacular
and the Biblical.

The city of Ghent was one vast factory. Ever since
the First Empire, the great textile manufactories had

increased and multiplied. This Belgian Manchester, a hive of mills, jeered at Antwerp, the Belgian Liverpool. Machinery had transformed Belgium. The country was so rich in workers that fresh supplies were always forthcoming. Goods could be produced at very low prices, and Belgian industrialists would only pay correspondingly low wages. The Congress for the betterment of conditions, which had met in 1852 and 1856, had vainly demanded reforms for women and children employed in factories. Mere babies of eight and nine were wheeled there in barrows, and set to work. If they fell asleep they were roused by having sponges of cold water thrown over them. The race was becoming exhausted; but the conservative bulldogs hung on tenaciously.

The situation was worse in Ghent than in any other part of Belgium, because the confluence of the Lys and the Scheldt, continued by a canal to Holland, had attracted so many workers that the city had become a veritable forest of chimneys. In 1859, one of the people, a consumptive called Emile Moyson, had founded a mutual relief society, with a president who wore striking regalia, and a banner bearing the device: "God and the Law." Nevertheless, when Proudhon made a tour of Belgium in 1862, he wrote: "There is not one Republican in ten thousand in Belgium. Socialists do not even exist."

Anseele became a Socialist, and as the Church was opposed to class warfare, he declared war on the Church. Societies were formed in the coal-mining districts of Charleroi and Liége. In 1877, Anseele founded a Flemish Socialist Party. The small, stocky figure of

the printer was to be seen in the company of journalists in the cafés; he held forth in the manner of Proudhon (to whom he owed much more than to Marx), and argued the philosophy of poverty over and over again.

From a printer he had become a journalist. In 1879 the Belgian Socialist Party came into being. Anseele announced the dawn of a new era, when workers would usurp the place of their masters, and would themselves spin—spin the shroud of Capitalism. His sombre voice seemed to echo from the catacombs of a far-off epoch, the epoch of the great demagogues of the thirteenth century, who had left so marked a trace on Ghent, Bruges and Ypres. The workers listened to him open-mouthed. When Leopold II visited Ghent in 1877, he was hissed in the streets.

The leaders of the Flemish Socialist Party were men of the people. Their first organization was a Bakers' Union with headquarters in the Marché au Fil. Anseele and his friends had read Zola, Victor Hugo, and above all, Eugène Sue. With this literary equipment, they founded the daily paper *Vooruit* (*Forward*). They next came into contact with young lawyers in Brussels who spoke to them of Karl Marx. Together they created the Belgian Labour Party in 1885. Anseele and his fellow citizens were the practical men of this party, and they were supported by a solid wall of co-operative societies. The intellectuals of the movement were led by Emile Vandervelde, who soon became leader of the whole Party.

Vandervelde was a barrister at the Brussels Bar, the son of a Liberal magistrate, who held advanced views.

He was born in 1864 in the Rue Keyenveld, in a room facing a house where cholera patients lay dying. Emile Vandervelde always prophesied the death of Capitalism with a macabre calm, even when Capitalism was thriving more lustily than ever. Perhaps this sinister twist was derived from that hour when the angels of life and death had brushed wings in the Rue Keyenveld. When he was seventeen, young Vandervelde affiliated himself with the Socialist Party and went to London, where he met Marx, who died in that year.

It was as freakish to be a Socialist during those unprogressive years in Brussels as to be a Saint Simonite, a Mormon, or a Protectionist. In 1894, however, Vandervelde was elected deputy by consistory suffrage. In that same year, he was elected by plural suffrage [1] to the Chamber, where he was the leader of a consolidated group of thirty-four deputies.

Meanwhile in Ghent, Anseele, with his small yet telling vocabulary, had been exhorting the soldiers to crush the priesthood, and had damned the King as a murderer. He was imprisoned. So was Louis de Brouckère. Hainault was in flames. The entire Walloon country read Depuisseaux' *Republican Catechism*. Auguste Beernaert, an extremely able Catholic minister, proposed a moderate reform in the suffrage, and the rioting simmered down. It was this reform which brought thirty-four Socialists, including Vandervelde, to the Chamber.

Three years later the contemporary historian Charles

[1] Two votes for heads of households and persons of importance.

1909—ALBERT ENTERS BRUSSELS
AFTER THE DEATH OF LEOPOLD II

Seignobos wrote that Belgium was "the stake in the struggle of the secular Republicans against the adherents of the Church and the Monarchy." And M. Seignobos was right; for the Socialist leaders had shown themselves Republican at heart—reformers of the suffrage rather than of society.

In the years that followed, Emile Vandervelde continued to publish brilliant commentaries on Karl Marx. But Anseele's co-operative societies had prospered greatly, and M. Vandervelde had to get along without his help: Anseele had become a capitalist. He spun and wove, as he had predicted in the heroic years; but the shroud, the famous shroud of Capitalism, had been forgotten.

And M. Vandervelde too had shifted his ground, as gradually became apparent. He still made the Chamber resound with Wagnerian declamations delivered in his beautiful baritone voice; for he was a fervent Wagnerite, and every speech he made began with a reference to the *Rhinegold* or the *Twilight of the Gods*. But his were only cerebral outbursts, his Socialism was only theoretical. He became a professor in the University of Brussels and President of the Internationale; he was a Germanophile, though he never spoke German; a Belgian Socialist, though he never spoke a word of Flemish. In 1910, King Albert knew as much about the Belgians and Belgian Socialism as he. This was the state of affairs on the eve of the War. The Socialists had concentrated entirely on the question of universal suffrage. And then the election of 1912 resulted in a crushing loss for the Left Wing. Contrary

to M. Vandervelde's advice, the Party had made open attacks on the Church. It was a bad move, and M. de Broqueville, the leader of the Right, had very cleverly taken advantage of their tactics.

On April 14, 1913, four hundred thousand Socialist workers "downed tools" at the bidding of their Republican leaders. In an over-populated country like Belgium, where villages are the size of towns, where cities are crowded together, and where one man in six is a factory worker, a word of command is quickly obeyed. In a forcible speech, M. Vandervelde had announced the general strike, "peaceful, formidable and inevitable." A speaker from the Right had replied, point for point: "If your strike is formidable, it will not be peaceful; if it is peaceful, it will not be formidable." This was excellent logic, but untrue in fact. Not a single window was broken, not a shot was fired.

Exactly a week later, M. Masson, a Liberal Deputy from Hainault, established an order for the day which, while condemning the strike, foreshadowed Constitutional revision as soon as "a system better than that in existence" should be found. M. Vandervelde was far too shrewd not to understand.

The battle was won. "It is a prize for good behaviour," said M. Brunet, the future President of the Chamber. M. de Broqueville had submitted to the King in confidence a scheme for universal suffrage, which applied to all male Belgians over the age of twenty-five.

M. Vandervelde issued a proclamation that was both triumphant and cautious. It stated: "Universal suffrage

is on its way." A wealthy bourgeois Deputy said aggressively: "Why don't they make him Minister without Portfolio at once!"

It was to take one more year and the German Ultimatum to bring about his appointment.

Flemish Socialism, as we have seen, became in time Belgian Socialism; an issue urban and secular; something to be dealt with by legislative action. But Flemish Nationalism remained, and became even more intensely, what it had been from the beginning—a temperamental issue, largely rural, religious and cultural. As such, it was something to be handled with gloves; with a sympathetic knowledge of the Flemish temper and tradition. This knowledge was often far to seek in the "official Belgium" of Brussels landowners, the Bourse, and M. Vandervelde. How then are we to understand the problem of Flemish Nationalism, as it stood when King Albert fell heir to it?

Let us turn for a moment to the cities of Flanders at the close of the eighteenth and the beginning of the nineteenth centuries. Everywhere we find vast, icy, patrician houses which bear witness to the persistence of social hierarchies. To judge from their dimensions, they fully occupied the time of innumerable servants. (In Belgium, servants are called *subjects.*) When the Empire was established, a fresh access of prosperity led to a vast increase in these mansions. The market which now opened in the south helped many manufacturers to amass large fortunes, and the Dutch domination (1815-1830) made them still wealthier. This was the country

of well-stocked cellars and handsome family jewels.
Every large household possessed a resident chaplain who
was shown every consideration. There was abundance
of good fare. I have by me some of the menus of the
time. They make my mouth water. At Courtrai, the
heirs of wealthy families were given presents of a million francs at Christmas. French was spoken at the New
Year festivities and at business meetings. It was a
peculiar brand of French, with queer intonations and
many mistakes. It was also full of picturesque twists,
happy phrases and archaisms.

Sometimes, in intimate gatherings, a little Flemish
would creep in. Nearly all diminutives, nicknames, ex-
clamations, oaths, all expressions of emotion and affection, all words pertaining to children and servants were
Flemish, but a bastard Flemish. The game-keeper's
vocabulary was spontaneously made use of when coverts
were being discussed, the coachman's jargon was adopted
when the conversation turned on horses. The Church
dignitaries spoke Flemish, but a mere formal Flemish
that was employed in the pulpit and the confessional.
No one perfected himself in that language; each and
all perfected themselves in French. No one would have
dared to speak Parisian French; that would have been
pedantic; but all made strenuous efforts to acquire the
polite air. To-day, the cultured Flamingant [1] does not
exist. If he were to revisit the earth, his cause would
be lost in advance. The good old Flemish language is
forgotten. It will not be long before its mangled remains are forgotten too.

[1] A partisan of "home rule" (Flamingantism) for Flanders.

Towards the year 1880, at the time when the first warning signs of militant Flamingantism appeared on the horizon, the middle classes and the aristocracy of Flanders had long since lost their Flemish. I have known families where mental slackness, combined with routine and prejudice, have gone so far that the children of a burgomaster who lived all the year round on their country estate could not understand a word the villagers said.

The founders of Independent Belgium came from the middle classes, and the whole of the Belgian nineteenth century was a bourgeois century. Only taxpayers were entitled to vote. It had occurred to none of the middle classes, Flemish or Walloon, to make Flemish an official language. It was only in the universities that philologists, who were greatly attracted by German science, upheld the rights of Flemish and Netherlandish literature. No one paid any attention to them, and the bourgeoisie looked on them as eccentrics. Flamingantism only came into being and developed along with Republicanism.

I remember the first partisans of Flamingantism, when they arrived in the large cities and proclaimed their grievances aloud. The majority of them were countryfolk, with black felt hats, beards, and spectacles. They held extraordinary confabulations in cheap cafés and taverns, where they behaved in the unruly and assertive manner of raw students fresh from their village homes. They brought out hundreds of pamphlets, discussed aesthetic freedom, and pasted up glaring posters which bore weird devices. Their password was the cry

of the seagull which heralds the storm, and this wailing bird which beats its wings above the canals of Antwerp and Ghent voiced fairly accurately what these fervent youths were trying to say. With their black and yellow posters, black and yellow flags, and black and yellow badges, they seemed to be wheeling round and round in circles in search of a new régime.

Their leader was a student from Roulers, Albrecht Rodenbach, who died when he was twenty-six. He was a connection of Georges Rodenbach, the Fransquillon [1] author of *Bruges the Dead*. Like the Maeterlincks and the Verhaerens, the Rodenbachs never heard any language but French in their own homes. But Albrecht was an original, an extraordinarily precocious boy, who, like Augustin Thierry, was fascinated by the Middle Ages. When he read Chateaubriand, he too must have repeated with the same gesture: "Pharamond, Pharamond, we have fought with swords. . . ."

The Flemings of the years between 1890 and 1900 suddenly acquired a passionate interest in belfries, crusades, communal battles, and the glory of the Flemish people. The popular novels of Henri Conscience had aroused a taste for reading in the Flemish population who, for many years, had scarcely opened a book. Conscience was a facile and extraordinarily prolific writer. Like Sir Walter Scott, he went back to the past; he reclothed in his own words the heroic history of Flanders. In particular he celebrated the Battle of Courtrai where, on July 11, 1302, the Flemish commoners had wiped out the cavalry of the King of France, and on the next

[1] A Fleming who had adopted French as his language.

day had hung six hundred golden spurs from the ceiling of the church of Notre Dame. Their banner was a black lion on a yellow ground. There was an instantaneous rage for this standard, the golden spurs and July 11. More or less unintentionally, Conscience had restored to Flanders a national day of rejoicing. Although he himself was no Flamingant and was French by birth, he became a symbolic ancestor of Flemish nationalism. Like the cult of Aryanism farther north, Flemish nationalism has always turned a blind eye to little anomalies of this sort.

Albrecht Rodenbach was fortunate enough to be numbered with the prophets who have died young. He left behind him a mediocre poem *Gudrun,* and a glamorous reputation that was a mixture of William Tell and O'Connell. His writings showed the influence of German thought; but from 1900 onward the Flemings were fermenting with an absolute fever for expansion, and were not critical. They demanded that education should be given entirely in Flemish, that they should have a Flemish University, and a Flemish autonomy— that is, if *Zelfbestuur* can be translated by the word autonomy. If we stick to the letter, we might say self-government. This expression summed up their entire doctrine.

However, there were still to be considered those authentic Flemings who only spoke French. To these the Flamingants said: "You are not Flemish. The long years of bondage have worn you out, degraded you, paled your colours. You will again become Flemish if you learn to speak your mother-tongue, the one,

the true, the only Flemish language. You are a base product of the cities; you have been imported like merchandise, or else you are merely a secondary species who do not even blush to think you have forgotten the poetry of your ancestors and their deeds of high renown. Soon you will be indistinguishable from the people of Brussels, those bastards, those caricatures of Parisians. The Flanders you speak of is nothing but a Flanders of historical processions and collected folklore. . . ."

To whom the Fransquillon Flemings replied: "We are even more Flemish than you. The story of the jongleurs and chroniclers, clerks and abbés, merchants and soldiers, who spoke the French language, as did Brunetto Latini, because it was the clearest and most convenient, goes back to the earliest centuries. You have a Mistral, the gentle and angelic Guido Gezelle—a poet, you say, like Goethe and Shelley, Anderson and Dante. Keep him. Found a Flemish University. Unearth the old manuscripts and books of the ancient story-tellers, but do not impose this language of country priests and peasants on us. Sing its praises, if you will, but do not attempt to establish it by law, any more than Provençal or Breton are established in France. . . ."

But as both sides claimed to be in the right, it was plain that they would one day come to blows; and the most fervent adherents of the seagull wound up by saying: "Your fine speeches are a waste of breath. If you want war, war it shall be, and as we are in the majority . . . We have no bone to pick with the Wal-

loons, who shall keep their mother-tongue. But we, the Flamingants, demand absolute rights for our own people under the slogan: *In Vlaanderen Vlaamsch*— Flemish in Flanders. Democracy is on our side. A day will come when the King will only speak to us in Flemish."

Thus the dispute continued, growing daily a little more venomous. The inhabitants of Antwerp were the most aggressive. Three deputies, Catholic, Liberal and Socialist, headed the campaign. All three were destined to become Ministers of the King. The people of Brussels and the bourgeoisie would have shuddered with horror had they but suspected that the King said to his personal friends: "I sympathize with these Flemings, though we must stop them from going too far. But in a land of liberty like ours, their cause is already won." At the Court Ball in 1911, he summoned M. Van Cauwelaert, a young deputy from Antwerp, the most violent and aggressive of all the new prophets, and spoke to him with noticeably marked understanding. He was no longer afraid of such innovations. He would have shrugged his shoulders had he been called a partisan of Flamingantism, because he disliked labels; but he had learnt Flemish, and he listened closely to the great wave of opinion which was rising in the villages of the Campine and the countryside of Bruges.

Danger threatened. The King was well aware that here, as in any militant expression of mass-sentiment, lurked an unknown and formidable element. Proud and turbulent to a degree, bitter and sensitive, like all the people of the Marches, the Flemish had never lost

their ingrained dread of what the morrow would bring
forth, nor their unconquerable fear of betrayal.   In all
their polemics, the word traitor recurred.   Yet the people of Brussels merely shrugged, and said: "It's impossible to argue with them. . . ."   The need of the hour
was not to argue with them, but to gain their confidence.

The Flemish asked, above all, for sympathy.   When
he reached Brussels, the young Flamingant deputy
with his glasses and long beard felt vaguely intimidated.
When he mixed with the world of officialdom, he became a prey to deep distrust which soon gave place to
sharp irritation.   During the *Te Deum* in St. Gudule,
he felt that everyone was staring at him when he made
responses in his own language, as if he had committed
a breach of etiquette.   As he was suffering then, so—
he felt—Flanders had always been made to suffer.   Flamingantism was soon exalted to a great and tragic
cause.   I had friends at college who used to pray to be
allowed to die for Flanders.

To crown all, the priests, peasant and mystic like
their Irish brethren, and always on the look-out for
fresh crusades, let loose their cohorts against impious
France and godless Wallonia.

In July, 1914, the voice of unrest swelled up from
the plain of Flanders.   It seemed certain that it would
be necessary to take a step forward on the road to reform before the winter of 1915, when the seagull would
wing its way back from the frozen seas to wail above
the quays at Antwerp.

CHAPTER IV

THE EVE OF WAR

BERLIN, 1913. Diplomatic life moved at a slow
pace, and the representatives of small powers were
kept at arm's length, like poor relations.

The Minister from Belgium was Baron Eugène Beyens. His mission to Berlin had been undertaken in
1912 at great sacrifice on his part; he had been one of
King Albert's Ministers since 1909, and had only accepted the appointment on the insistence of his royal
master, who rightly deemed that he was the man best
fitted to succeed Baron Greindl. The latter had allowed himself to be misled by all the siren-songs that
echoed in the Wilhelmstrasse.

Jules Cambon, then French Ambassador, soon perceived that here was a valuable colleague. Baron Beyens, who was an ardent Catholic and deeply attached to
all the traditions of his country; Baron Beyens, whom
Cambon called Monsieur de Beyens, was not the man
to be lightly swayed. He took a magnificent house in
the Jaegerstrasse, which contained one of the finest col-
lections of bronzes in Europe, and immediately let it
be seen that he was going to live up to his position.
He was greatly attracted by the powerful Jews, and soon
became their friend, treating them exactly as he treated
the gentlemen of the Wilhelmstrasse. He was particularly attached to Kederlen, whom he had known in

Roumania. Although he was a brilliant writer, he wrote little. He was the diplomat who gathered his own information, locked himself in his room, and drew up an elegant report for his Government. He would lay it aside for twenty-four hours, and not till this interval had elapsed would he send it to Brussels. His dry and authoritative manner inspired his younger colleagues with terror. Certain French deputies had said to Cambon: "You will soon have him under your thumb," but Cambon was too subtle and perceptive to have any illusion on this score.

Baron Beyens belonged to that category of Parisian-ized Belgians who distrust France. When all the motives that caused Belgium to be suspicious of Germany were enumerated to him, he would retort with a recital of French political chicanery, from the time of Prince de Polignac and his great Plan of 1830 down to the policy of M. Joseph Caillaux. He was not yet sure of Germany's good intentions, but so strongly did he desire to believe in them that he gladly accepted anything that would lend weight to his theory.

Halfway through 1913, Baron Beyens expressed the hope that the King would come to Germany to review the regiment of Luneberg Dragoons, of which he was honorary colonel. Albert weighed the idea carefully, finally decided to accept the invitation, and took advantage of it to tour Germany. A Berlin tailor made him a Dragoon uniform; the blue coat was so becoming that the King said to his officers: "No uniform has ever suited me better." The enormous collar rose up to his ears. The German army was gratified by the Sover-

eign's visit. There were more Germans than ever in Antwerp. The King went first to Hamburg, where he had a long interview with Ballin. The famous ship-owner, who was a friend of the Kaiser, interested him greatly, and he overwhelmed him with questions. He then continued on his way to Luneberg.

Luneberg is a small town in Hanover, the country of horse-breeding farmers, where the earth is so easily turned that ploughs can be drawn by horses of fairly light breed. The country provided excellent cavalry mounts; and as the regiment was recruited locally, the Hanoverian farmers served in the dragoon squadrons of their fathers, riding on horses that they themselves had bred. The organization had a character of its own, somewhat similar to that of a British territorial regiment. When the soldiers had served their time, they would re-visit the barracks to talk to their comrades and make a round of the stables. The N.C.O.'s were a very good lot, and the atmosphere was friendly.

Albert was received at the Hôtel de Ville by the Burgomaster, who wore a frock-coat and looked like Franz-Joseph. The King reviewed his regiment, and was present at the manœuvres. The men were magnificent, and their drilling superb. Major de Jonghe d'Ardoye and Captain de Bliquy, both officers in the Guides, who accompanied the King, were amazed. The silver used by the officers was engraved with the arms of the King. During mess, Albert spoke to everyone and had everything explained to him.

Next day, accompanied by his two officers, he left

for Potsdam. He was about to experience one of the most tragic days of his reign.

Wilhelm II received him warmly, with a loquacity that bordered on hysteria. This talkativeness did not trouble the King—it enabled him to remain silent, a state which he definitely preferred. The passing of the years had sharpened the contrast between them. Albert had grown more and more thoughtful; Wilhelm less and less so. Albert loathed self-display; Wilhelm was an exhibitionist. Albert disliked pomp and panoply; Wilhelm would change his uniform half a dozen times during the course of an official day. They strolled through the very ordinary gardens together, and the King was embarrassed when the Kaiser boasted of them. There were a few sickly-looking plants in the conservatories, to which Wilhelm proudly drew his attention. Had they been in his own greenhouses at Laeken, Albert would either not have noticed them, or would have ordered them to be flung on to the rubbish-heap. He listened without the flicker of an eyelash. His officers bit their lips to keep back their laughter. Presently they came to the tomb of Frederick II, and as they stood in front of the mausoleum, the Emperor said in a smothered voice: "Only to think that in 1806, the French swine stabled their horses here!" The King continued to smile courteously.

Two great dinners were given at which the élite of Berlin society were present. The first was a dazzling affair. The King, his two officers, Baron Beyens and Major de Melotte, the Military Attaché, were the only

Belgians present. It was very warm, and Berlin was delightful in the soft, springlike atmosphere. The table was a bed of violets. Baron Beyens, who was on the Emperor's right, openly praised his eloquence and his wonderful memory for names, places and dates.

Fifty-five guests attended the second dinner held in the jasper banqueting-hall. The Emperor was in the uniform of a colonel of the Household Hussars, with the Grand Cordon of Leopold, Albert in that of a colonel of Dragoons, with the Black Eagle. The same guests were present, but with the addition of Bethmann-Hollweg, Tirpitz, Falkenhayn and Moltke, all the War Lords—a galaxy of celebrated names. Beyens was surprised at the King's abstracted air. Accustomed as he was to Albert's temperamental fits of depression, he had never seen him so melancholy in so brilliant a company. On the contrary, such a varied and interesting gathering usually took him out of himself. "That night the King sat between the Empress and Princess Augusta," writes the Baron; "he spoke in German to the gaily-smiling Empress, and to the Princess, who was so ignorant of our country that she actually believed the members of our Royal Family always spoke to one another in German. . . ."

At eleven o'clock the King took his leave. His official visit was now over, but he wished to spend a day in Berlin, and had engaged a suite at the Adlon. Wilhelm II continued to hold forth, but no longer about politics. The King had had a long talk with Moltke. As he left, he had said to his Minister: "Come to the

hotel to-morrow morning at nine o'clock. I want to talk to you."

Undoubtedly, there was thunder in the air. The Emperor laughed louder and louder. Commander du Roy noticed that he thumped Moltke violently on the back, and reflected that such manners differed vastly from those of the Court of Brussels.

The next morning proved to be one of the turning-points of Albert's reign. He had risen very early, and had gone out alone into the Linden gardens. When Beyens arrived at the Adlon, the King was just coming in from his walk, and as soon as he saw his Minister he suggested another stroll. In the walks of the public gardens, whose silence was only broken at that hour by the chirping of birds and muffled clip-clop of horses' hoofs, the King described his interview with Wilhelm II on the previous night.

The Emperor had made a long anti-French disquisition. In the familiar and condescending tones he used when addressing his outpourings to his royal cousin, he had laid bare to him certain schemes. The King had at first believed them to be no more than those verbal explosions of which the Kaiser had already given samples. At the last Court Ball, for instance, he had harangued the Belgian Minister and his friend, Baron Lambert, and had broken out into denunciations of France, the sole cause of all the trouble in Europe. Further, at this same Court Ball, as the Crown Prince was walking arm-in-arm with von Kluck, he had said in a very loud voice: "That's the general who will lead the offensive on Paris." But were these objectionable

outbursts merely the result of that itch to talk from which the Emperor suffered? The King knew Wilhelm too well to lay overmuch stress on his infuriating digressions. He had experienced several of them since the beginning of his reign.

But this time it was serious—so serious that inwardly Albert was appalled. Under Bethmann-Hollweg, the Kaiser was renewing the promise he had made to Leopold II under von Bülow: the promise to extend the frontiers of Belgium if she would give free passage to the German army on its march on Paris. Should war break out, Belgian neutrality would be violated.

The King, who was now very composed, at length had the evidence; and he who had so often hesitated when difficulties arose was in full possession of himself now that there was no other voice than the voice of duty. In these stark circumstances, he saw himself instantly as Head of the State, and quickly communicated his decisions. Baron Beyens must see M. Cambon with the least possible delay, and acquaint him with the integral facts of the Kaiser's conversation. M. Cambon was charged not to mention the matter, except to M. Poincaré, to whom he was to speak in the strongest possible terms. What would normally have been an indiscretion now became a precaution for the safety of Europe. If Wilhelm II had thought that his bursts of eloquence could shake the resolution of a Belgian King—if he had believed he could drag Albert into the German orbit, he was vastly mistaken. On the contrary, his ill-advised action had been a grave diplomatic

error; for this conversation was to give rise to a new order of things.

Cambon has narrated these events in detail. A new era in the conjoint history of Belgium and France came into being. The King was not Francophile by instinct; he had inherited the old antipathy of his predecessors for all that recalled Napoleon III. It was Wilhelm who finally scotched this distrust.

Thus was brought about a great reversion in Belgian policy. Two worlds, two human conceptions had come into contact at the violet-strewed table at Potsdam, and the brightest fact that emerged from this momentous meeting was that the hero of to-morrow was already bearing himself as a statesman.

He was in his thirty-ninth year, the age when those whose dreams are still unrealized watch with agony the slow trickling of the years. Now that he was thirty-nine, the King felt that his destiny was taking a tragic turn. In his own country, however, he was able to carry on—more, to build up. He was master of himself. A general strike had ended in smoke. Social reforms had been duly instituted. His reign, in the popular view, was progressing happily. Belgium would always be the country of factory chimneys and giant furnaces, with powerful colonies of Germans in Antwerp, and great banking houses. The King would live to a good old age, give his patronage to seats of learning and charitable organizations; he would be enlightened and beneficent, a devout Catholic and a humanitarian ruler, possessing the necessary discretion to hold the acrimoni-

ous clergy in check and keep the statisticians of the
Solvay Institute within bounds. During his reign, there
would be many debates on Free Trade, the distribution
of production, and the adjustment of wages in proportion to work. Missionaries in the Congo would listen
to him eagerly. Albert I would be the Benefactor and
the Economist.

No one ever wondered whether he had courage. It
was supposed that he had—but was much courage
needed by a King of the Belgians? So ran the thoughts
of the average Belgian at the beginning of 1914.

The Season in Brussels that winter was exceptionally
brilliant. Trade was flourishing, and no shadow of
foreboding clouded the minds of the people whose
chosen spheres of activity were factories and banks. A
Court Ball was given, and two Drawing Rooms were
held. The new Republic of China sent over a special
mission, and dancing took place "in the gardens illuminated with Chinese lanterns, all the Belgian Ministers wearing oriental decorations lavishly distributed by
the Chinese Ambassador." Brussels was enjoying itself.
The Dresden Opera Company gave the whole of Wag-
ner's *Ring* at the Monnaie; "during the interval, the
audience dined in the restaurant, and a horn sounded
the Siegfried motif to announce the lifting of the curtain. . . ." The Queen was more and more interested
in music. The King conscientiously attended every
function. The Princes were growing up. Lieutenant
de Neve de Roden was aide-de-camp to the Duke of
Flanders, while Major de Groote had replaced Captain
Maton in that capacity with the Duke of Brabant. The

King had wrenched his shoulder as the result of a fall in the Forest of Soignes. He appeared at the Court Ball with his arm in a black silk sling.

The first death took place in the family: the Countess of Flanders died, beloved and mourned by all, and the King's subjects who knew how dearly he had loved her, were able to gauge his grief. Notwithstanding, the Queen ended the season by giving a garden party at Laeken. The revival of military enthusiasm had again made uniform the vogue. Young men of fashion anticipated conscription by joining the Guides. They were to be gazetted second Lieutenants in August. . . . The Jesuits of St. Michel were cramming candidates for the Military School. The star of the Baron de Broqueville was at its zenith. Aviation was attracting young officers. Pégoud and Clieslaegers set up records. Brand Whitlock, the new United States Ambassador, had just arrived. Count von Below-Saleske, his German colleague, who had a house in the Rue Belliard, had brought back from China a silver goblet riddled by a rebel's bullet. When he showed it to his guests, he said: "I have never held any post where there were not a few disturbances—there was the Revolution in Turkey and the Boxer Rising in China. I am a bird of ill-omen. Now I am resting. Nothing ever happens in Brussels."

The conservatories at Laeken were lovelier than ever. At the Horse Show there were scarcely any carriages, and Leopold II's stables had been turned into garages. The King and Queen of Denmark paid an official visit. Seated on a balcony the two Queens watched a parade

in the Avenue de Tervueren. The two Kings, both of
them of gigantic stature, were on horseback. Albert I
wore a black tunic and white buckskin breeches; Christian was in scarlet, with a bearskin on his head. In the
evening, Heldy sang and Ysaye conducted the second
act of *Orpheus* in the small theatre at Laeken. The
Royal children "clung to their mother in the Royal Box
and fidgetted with boredom." On this unforgettable
night, the curtain went up on a dimly-lighted stage;
the ballet from La Monnaie looked like a classic frieze
in the amethystine shadows. "The rhythmic cadence
of the solemn measure will always recall that summer
night, those gossamer shades from which Eurydice can
nevermore be snatched. . . ."

At the Hôtel de Ville, M. Max had arranged a décor
that had all the enchantment of a fairy-tale—a fit setting
for those days of high festival. There was a divertisse-
ment by Croisa and the ballerinas; there was the triumphal procession which wended its way through the
Grand' Place while the heralds, blowing their Theban
trumpets, preceded the Kings on their caparisoned
steeds. Rarely had Brussels been more resplendent.
Cardinal Mercier created a sensation whenever he appeared. At the theatre on gala nights the people, in
a frenzy of excitement, pointed out to each other the
lions of the day—John d'Oultremont, Georges de Ligne,
Lambert Rothschild, the Sinceys, Villalobar, the d'Aren-
bergs—and many other gallant figures soon, alas, to
be mowed down by the scythe of Death. Brussels was
a reincarnation of what it had been on the eve of Waterloo.

At the beginning of July the Season ended, and society left town. One morning the *haute monde* squeezed into the church of St. Jacques at Coudenburg, around a black pall spangled with silver. The Nuncio officiated. At the conclusion of the service the congregation surrounded Count Clary and Aldringen, the Austro-Hungarian Minister, in mourning for the Archduke Franz Ferdinand, who had been assassinated at Serajevo. On the day of the tragedy, Count Clary had been present at a ceremony at Belœil where the centenary of the Prince de Ligne was being celebrated. Jules Déstree, the Socialist deputy, had made an admirable speech.

July 21, the anniversary of the Monarchy, was a strange day. The King had just returned from Ostend, bronzed by the sea air but looking troubled. The Queen and the Princess were radiant. The Princes were dressed in grey satin with muslin collars. The choir of St. Gudule sang magnificently. On either side of the crimson carpet a double line of Grenadiers presented arms. After the service, carriage doors were slammed and the escort of Guides galloped up the Treurenberg, advanced along the Rue Royale, and formed up in front of the Palace. The carriages disappeared under the arches. The King wore his black uniform with epaulettes, the dress uniform of peace . . . for the last time.

The aide-de-camp and the colonel in command of the escort raised their swords in salute. The regiment returned to its headquarters at Etterbeek. An era had come to an end.

CHAPTER V

BERLIN, LONDON, BRUSSELS; OR THE IRON DICE

IN Berlin the drama was approaching its climax. Up to the very last moment, Baron Beyens continued to hope, as those in Brussels continued to hope. Mobilization had altered the aspect of the city. For the first time, it had changed colour: it had been metamorphosed by the field-grey. The diplomats had never seen this war array, and no longer recognized the youth of Germany. During the summer months, many of the wives of foreign statesmen had returned to their own countries. The grass-widowers dined at the Kaiserhof, the Adlon, or the Bristol, which were crowded with officers. The most prominent young men in Berlin society suddenly appeared clad in the famous field-grey. It seemed as though a new race had come forth from the bowels of the earth. With the full consciousness of duty done, Jules Cambon was the star of these gatherings, the most sought-after and scintillating guest.

As soon as the news of the German Ultimatum was known, Baron Beyens wired to Brussels: "Gloomy rumours about Belgium. I advise that the army be ready. . . ." He had learnt at the Bristol of the violation of the Grand Ducal frontier. Occasionally, a fanfare was heard as the Kaiser's carriage drove past. A number of Belgians in Berlin rushed to the Legation and asked for passports. No one had ever worried

about passports before. The Legation hummed like a beehive. The most persistent visitors were the Belgian prostitutes in Berlin, whose civil status was extraordinarily difficult to define.

On Monday, as a harbinger of what was to come, diplomats were forbidden by telephone to speak in any other language than German. The people themselves, the majority of whom were Socialists, remained fairly quiet but were beginning to show signs of excitement. It was learnt that at Munich the crowd had sacked the French and Russian Legations. The Belgian Minister went to interview Jagow. In the antechamber, he met Herr von Lerchenfeld, the Bavarian Minister at Potsdam, who said: "France and Russia are not prepared for war, while Germany is overwhelmingly powerful. We must take advantage of the position. We will win the war whatever it may cost us. . . ." This was indeed an admission.

That very hour, Germany declared war on Belgium. At seven o'clock that evening, Baron Beyens was at the Adlon. An urgent message recalled him to the Legation. Brussels had sent the news of the catastrophe by secret cypher, which M. Peltzer had de-coded.

On the next day, Baron Beyens went to von Jagow at 8 A.M., and challenged him point-blank. Thus cornered, the Secretary of State admitted: ". . . a rapid transit through Belgium is a matter of life or death to us . . . as a private individual, I can understand your answer. As Secretary of State, I cannot voice an opinion." Baron Beyens closed the interview by saying icily: "You will not take Liége as easily as you think,

and you will find yourself confronted by England."

That evening the *Berliner Tageblatt,* unknown to the Government, issued a special edition with the news that Great Britain had declared war. The crowd made for Sir Edward Goschen's Embassy, and would have wrecked it had not the police intervened. Herr Zimmermann handed the English and Belgian Ambassadors their passports. He looked wretched, and made no attempt to justify himself. Friends of both Ambassadors voiced their genuine regret—the regret of men of the world who were also straightforward and sincere. The people had gone mad. The streets were alive, seething like a witch's cauldron stirred by some shadowy demon. Frenzied crowds thronged the city, and so complete was their ignorance that they cheered wildly outside the Japanese Embassy, believing Japan to be an ally of Germany against Russia.

The personnel of the British Embassy and the Belgian Legation were conducted to the station under strong escort at an early hour in the morning. Only milkmen were abroad, and the precaution was quite unnecessary. All were perfectly calm. Major de Melotte alone caused a diversion by his outbreaks. Ever since the previous night, he had asseverated that if he should see the Kaiser riding on horseback Unter den Linden, he would fling himself at the horse's bridle and create an uproar. It had taken endless trouble to dissuade him.

A special train was under the command of a Colonel of the Reserve. It moved off in deathly silence. Suddenly, Major de Melotte's wife, unnerved by the strain

of the last few days, burst into tears. Baron Beyens muttered from his corner: "Weeping women . . . the last straw. . . ." They passed trains packed with reservists carrying wreaths of evergreen, and shouting that they were off on a pleasure-trip to Paris. It was a stifling hot afternoon. When they reached Minden, Red Cross nurses, who were drawn up on the platform, came up to the windows of the train and shrieked insults at them like the "petroleuses" of the Commune. At length they crossed the frontier. The Dutch station-master gave them the first news of the offensive on Liége, and the heroic defence by the King and his army. Goschen strode over to his Belgian colleague, and grasped him warmly by the hand.

On August 3, Chancellor Bethmann-Hollweg, in the uniform of a Major General, outlined the policy of Germany in the white hall of the Reichstag and announced the violation of the Belgian frontier: "This act is a breach of international law: the wrong we thereby commit, we will try to make good as soon as our military aims have been attained. . . ." When Sir Edward Goschen, certain at last of the decision of his Government, had sought out the Chancellor and coldly explained to him the *casus belli,* Bethmann was distracted. Goschen had never yet seen him excited or moved. Bethmann approached him trembling, and stammered: "You would never do that . . . for a scrap of paper."

Jagow, that Parisianized old diplomat, confessed to a deputy of the Reich: "I have no heart for this busi-

ness," and von Bülow, the ex-Chancellor, deliberately recorded this incident in his memoirs. In all conscience, the Germans used every means in their power, even their candour, to stress the heinousness of their crime.

And so, amidst general confusion, this most macabre of comedies reached its end. The officials of the Wilhelmstrasse had completely lost their heads. Queries were despatched from department to department. In the disorder that prevailed, each turned on his nearest neighbour. One of the administratives exclaimed to the special correspondent of the *Journal des Débats:* "You are to blame for what is happening." The power had so completely passed into the hands of the military faction that those in civil ranks were helpless. It was a far cry from Prince von Bismarck and his great school of double-dealing. German writers set themselves to the task of forging a link between the two epochs. The heads of departments resigned. Only the General Staff counted, and the General Staff's sole preoccupation was to hasten the offensive. Bureaucrats were aghast at the unforeseen proportions which the adventure had assumed. All was over. The iron dice had been thrown.

Four years earlier, Wilhelm II, in dress uniform, had arrived at the Gare du Nord at Brussels, and had driven up the Boulevard Botanique in the King's car. With what curiosity mingled with admiration the people had gazed at him then. The political world, carried away by the rhetoric of the All Highest, had spoken of him as the master of Europe, a maker of history. No man had seemed more marked out than he to shape events

and bend them to his will. Helmeted, clad in resplendent uniform, he had made a striking figure; and they had thought that, should a war break out, he alone would regulate its course—that the best thing Belgian officers could do would be to follow the lessons of the Kriegs Akademie of Berlin. He had spoken of all things to all men, launched ships and reviewed armies. Whosoever should not be for him should be against him. That famous day on which the die should be cast would be *his* day—*der Tag*.

But on August 4, 1914, Wilhelm II had played out his part. For another four years, he would be seen going from one Headquarters to another, a mere puppet in the hands of Hindenburg and Ludendorff, until the final desertion and his shameful exile. On the same fourth of August a shell burst on the Belgian frontier near Liége. Trooper Fonck of the Second Lancers was killed. With the bursting of this shell, Albert I made his entrance into history.

How different was the traditional attitude of England. There had been no formal promise, but there was the certainty of a fundamental sympathy. Great Britain was slow indeed to come to a decision, but that decision was ultimately reached. Going back through the ages, Albert remembered how first the Plantagenets, and then the Lancastrians and Yorkists, had watched jealously over the plains of Flanders. When the Dukes of Burgundy became invaders, Bruges and Antwerp became danger points. With its knowledge of bygone history, the Foreign Office had long been obsessed with

the necessity of protecting Belgian soil from aggressors, whether they came from the south or the east. This psychology was manifested during the reign of Louis XIV, that era when "the members of the House of Commons would rather have sold their shirts than have allowed France to conquer the Low Countries."

The members of the French Convention, who were new to international affairs, burdened Jacobin France with a crushing inheritance by deliberately ignoring England's attitude. They bequeathed Antwerp to her. Napoleon, through his inability to refuse this conquest of the tri-colour, was forced into war, and going from victory to victory, was driven to the final catastrophe. After successive coalitions, Wellington at length consented to land his grenadiers in Belgium. The treaty which followed was particularly severe on France. It committed one mistake, however—it established Prussia on the left bank of the Rhine. Amongst the official documents, the King now came across Castlereagh's opinion:

"I have not lost sight of the fact that there may be some danger in establishing a Power that is essentially military, and in consequence, to some slight extent aggressive, in such close contact with the Low Countries and Holland. But it is a secondary danger to which we must not sacrifice our principal object, that of opposing the designs of France. . . ."

The structure crashed to the ground in 1830, when Belgium freed herself from the overlordship of Holland and upheld her claim to self-government. The Court of St. James did not interfere so long as no change took

place on the French frontiers. Like France, England
preferred the moral barrier of neutrality to violent solu-
tions. Five Powers—England, France, Austria, Prussia
and Russia—solemnly guaranteed this neutrality. On
the eve of 1870, conscious of the thunder in the air, the
Court of St. James confirmed its first intentions by signing a special treaty. This stated that Great Britain
would send her naval and military forces against which-
ever of the two belligerent countries—France or Germany—dared to violate the Belgian frontier. This resolute action sufficed to deflect the German menace from
Belgium.

How ardently, in 1913, the King of the Belgians
had longed to see history repeat itself. He knew only
too well what a terrifying effect a single word from
London might produce on the agitated and changeable
world of Berlin. Since 1905, Colonel Bridges and
Colonel Barnardiston, the military attachés in Brussels,
had discussed the outlook with the Belgian Staff. But
on all sides, statesmen preserved the silence of the grave.

The man to whom Providence had confided the destiny of the British Empire was unquestionably the last
person in England to make a rapid decision. It was
for Sir Edward Grey to say "No" to Germany before any
blood was shed. He was a landed proprietor and aristocrat, a devout Churchman, and a great lover of nature;
fifteen years later, he was to co-operate in the work of
protecting the flora and fauna of the Congo, which had
been undertaken by King Albert. As often happens
to the sons of old and distinguished families, he had
entered politics as a matter of course. Able, but devoid

of originality, Sir Edward's chief tenet was never to bind England to any country in Europe. His motto might have been: "I will make no promises, but I will always keep my word."

This is all very well between gentlemen, but it is worse than useless between gentlemen and gangsters. Towards 1912, when Lichnowsky, the German Ambassador, managed to extort a letter from him which stated that England was not bound to France, Sir Edward regretted it to such an extent that he hastened to assure Paul Cambon over and over again that neither was England bound to Germany. It was he who authorized the discussions between the French and English Staffs, initiated by Colonel Repington. Sir Edward also permitted Colonel Barnardiston to speak, but he himself emphasized the fact that the conference "had no more significance than a discussion between the Westminster Fire Brigade and the Metropolitan Water Board."

Sir Edward had travelled very little, and had read very few books, but he knew to a nicety what public opinion and the House of Commons wanted. For the moment, he left Providence to carry on, and buried himself in the study of bird life and fly-fishing.

In June, 1914, Captain Maton, the Belgian Military Attaché in London, was invited to spend a week-end at Aldershot with General Sir Douglas Haig, who showered questions on him. The Belgian officer had already had an important interview with Major-General Sir Henry Wilson, Head of the War Office. The future Field-Marshal had pinned a huge map on the wall, on which

were marked in red all possible lines of invasion which the German armies might take on their march to Paris, including the route north of the Meuse. "Your Luxembourg has been described to me as an impenetrable labyrinth," he said. "I have been through it from end to end. The German army could cross it at its ease. There is water in every village."

Meanwhile, Sir Edward Grey had made no move. His disbelief in the possibility of war was so strong that he refused to suspect its existence in the minds of others. He was as straightforward as King Albert; he carried out his duty, but lacked all inspiration.

Sunday, August 2, 1914, was a day of brilliant sunshine. The people of Brussels had left the city *en masse*. There were far fewer cars than there are to-day. The good people of Brussels spent much shorter holidays, and went less far afield. They preferred the Forest of Soignes to the sea. Brussels was suffocatingly hot, almost deserted. It was like an English Sunday afternoon. Contrary to rule, the Foreign Office and the War Office had remained open. Viscount Davignon was seated in his big room at Number 8, whose windows overlooked the gardens of the Houses of Parliament. Count Leo d'Ursel was working in the adjacent room. The Premier, M. de Broqueville, a senator from Verviers, a great landowner who was respected throughout the country, was the calmest and most cautious man in the Ministry. In him were to be found all the wary and scrupulous traditions of Belgian diplomacy. It was a negative kind of diplomacy that walked delicately, al-

THE KING FLEW HIS OWN PLANE

ways anxious to please, involving itself in as many complications in the fulfilment of its undertakings as the Machiavellis usually employ in breaking them.

At half-past six the German Legation rang up. Herr von Below-Saleske wished an interview with the Minister. Herr von Below was a tall, elegant man, of whom common report said much that was good and much that was bad. He was a bachelor and, on the whole, nothing very much was known about him in Brussels, where it had not been possible to take his measure during the six months of his residence. At seven o'clock to the minute, his car drew up before the door of Number 8. A manservant in livery opened the door on which a crowned eagle was emblazoned. Herr von Below crossed the courtyard. Preceded by an official, he went upstairs. He walked quickly, with a nervous yet decided step. A messenger informed M. de Bassompierre and M. de Gaiffier, the Chief of Department and assistant Chief of Department, who were waiting in their offices.

The door of the Minister's room closed.

Viscount Davignon was conscious of the approaching storm.

"I came upstairs too quickly. . . . I shall be all right in a minute," murmured Herr von Below.

Then, in a firm voice he continued: "I have a confidential communiqué to hand over to you in the name of my Government."

As he spoke, he drew the Ultimatum from his pocket. M. Davignon rapidly read it through. It was in German. At last the fatal paper had seen daylight, as though

it were weary of its secret so long cherished. In spite
of the evidence before him, M. Davignon stammered:
"No—I can't believe it—it's . . . it's impossible—"

The two men stared at each other. The paper, the
famous scrap of paper, had fluttered to the ground between them, and lay at their feet.

The German diplomat felt that the comedy of emotion had lasted long enough. In a resolute voice, he
took up the tenor of the note, stressed its confidential
nature, confirmed his country's desire for peace, and
reiterated the news of an offensive against France that
was timed to take place almost immediately in the vicinity of Namur. Then, when he had delivered himself
of his principal business, he went on to the details, obtained a promise that the matter should immediately be
discussed at a meeting of the Ministers, listened in
silence to the horrified reply of M. Davignon, bowed,
bowed again and took his leave.

A telephone message was sent to M. de Broqueville,
but he could not be reached. A messenger, who was
despatched in haste, found the Premier on his doorstep
with his Secretary, the young Count de Lichtervelde.
They were going to dine together at the Provençaux in
the Rue Royale. The Premier betrayed no sign of his
feelings; he went straight to M. Davignon, heard what
he had to say, listened to the first sentences which M. de
Bassompierre had translated, and seated himself in an
armchair with extraordinary calm. M. de Bassompierre
was nervous. M. de Gaiffier and M. d'Ursel helped him.

It took them half an hour to agree on the exact trans-
lation. The German sentences were involved. I have

before me at this moment the celebrated memorandum written by M. de Bassompierre. Dozens of words are scored out. M. de Bassompierre read it slowly and distinctly. Eight o'clock struck in a silence like that of the grave.

When he had finished, M. van der Elst, the Secretary General, said to the Premier:

"Well, Monsieur, are we prepared?"

"Yes," answered M. de Broqueville, "the mobilization is proceeding without a hitch. The army will be ready to march to-morrow night . . . to-morrow morning even, if it were absolutely necessary . . . but there is a *but*. We have no heavy artillery. . . ."

They continued to talk for a few moments. It was now ten past eight. M. de Broqueville left the Ministry hurriedly, ran across the courtyard, jumped into his car, and said abruptly to his chauffeur:

"To the Palace."

Three staff officers were on duty at the Palace—Major Preudhomme, Major Galet and Major Davreux. The two latter had been marked out by destiny, one to be Commander-in-Chief, the other to be killed in battle. The Premier was ushered in immediately. The interview was very short. Neither the King nor the statesman ever breathed a word of what passed. At its conclusion, orders were given that all the ministers and statesmen were to meet at nine o'clock. At that moment, M. Jules Ingenbleek was leaving M. Paul Hymans's charming little house in the Rue Ducale. The King's secretary had just come in to offer his official con-

gratulations in the name of his royal master to the new Minister. They were talking quietly. "I have just seen the Premier drive up to the Palace," said M. Ingenbleek. "I suppose he is going to inform His Majesty of the outcome of the interview between Herr von Below and M. Davignon. You know, I suppose, that he asked for an audience a short while ago. I think it must have been similar to that which M. Klobukowsky had yesterday. I am sure that everything will be all right. Fortunately . . ."

Thus, the Ultimatum came like a bolt from the blue. Even those who had foreseen it would not as yet believe in it. For the first time, the classic argument was heard: "The Germans are dangerous, but they are not maniacs." It was also the most comforting form of argument. Within a stone's throw of the Palace the crowded restaurants rang with cheerful laughter. All the way from the Bois de La Cambre to the lower end of the city the trams were packed. The cinemas in the Rue Neuve were filling up. The aspect of Brussels was far more provincial then than it is to-day. In the Bois, violins were beginning to strike up in the cafés. So the gay strains of the orchestra herald the raising of the curtain on a great drama. Peace had become such a deep-rooted habit that the whole world still believed itself to be the audience even though the tragedy had ceased to be enacted on a stage, had invaded the auditorium itself, and had stalked abroad into the city and the country. Only one night was left to them before they would awaken from their idyll—they would rub their eyes, heavy with sleep, and behold the evidence of War.

The King went into the gardens of the Palace. His
aides-de-camp saw him striding up and down, a prey
to cold fury. In such moments, his lower lip would
quiver in a curious manner. Nothing but indignation
could cause this man, who was utterly fearless, to trem-
ble.

Without delay, M. de Bassompierre and M. de Gaiffier
had addressed themselves to the task of formulating the
reply.

The Ministers, the Commander-in-Chief, the Second
in Command and the Inspector General of the Artillery
were ushered into the presence of the King at half-past
nine. The whole staff of the Palace, in their scarlet
livery, were drawn up in the hall. Officials came and
went. The Ministers ascended the great stairway.
Major Galet said nothing, and Davreux kept on re-
peating: "We shall fight, we shall fight . . ." to an in-
visible interlocutor. The word "War" was incessantly
on the lips of all. The Ministers seated themselves
without formality, their chairs ranged round a red carpet. The King, wearing uniform, stern, impassive, took
his place in their midst, facing M. de Broqueville.
Through the windows, they could see the great chestnut-
trees of the Park and the eighteenth century belfry of
St. Jacques. M. Davignon read the document. He was
requested to read it a second time. When he had finished, M. de Broqueville asked permission to speak,
and gave his opinion.

The next morning, Tuesday, at six o'clock, Count
von Below sent a note from his Government stating
that "Germany would take by force what was refused

her." Albert wired to the King of England at ten
o'clock. At the same hour, he mounted his horse and
rode to the Chamber.

It must be recognized that in this solemn moment
the sky had suddenly lightened for the King. What
would he have done if France had adopted an attitude
similar to Germany's—if Belgium had been forced
to defend her two frontiers simultaneously? Instead of
being harried by doubts, torn between two decisions,
his road lay straight before him. His Ministers instantly grasped what was in his mind.

Meanwhile, when M. Ingenbleek, overwhelmed by
the tragic news, rushed in to see Major Galet, the King's
military spokesman and close friend, he found him
seated at his desk.

"Well, what do you think of it?" he burst out.

Major Galet showed no signs of tension or anxiety.
"I'm damn glad . . ." he replied.

"What!"

"I'm damn glad . . . now I know where I am."

The curt phrase expressed the general feeling. At
last Belgium knew where her duty lay. Now that the
real enemy had unmasked his batteries, all that remained was to fight.

On that Tuesday morning, when Brussels and the
countryside were waking, the King was finishing a solemn note to the Kaiser. It was the final and supreme
protest of outraged honour. He wrote it in French
and passed it to the Queen, who quickly translated it

into German in her bold handwriting. Both knew now where they were, too.

Now we are no longer dealing with history—we have come to the Golden Legend of our time. As on the day of the coronation, the Queen entered the Chamber, dressed in dark blue and wearing a hat with white feathers. She acknowledged the cheers of the deputies with deep curtseys, and seated herself in a gilded arm-chair. All the benches were crowded to overflowing. In the lobby many of the deputies were in uniform. Amongst them was Sergeant Hubin, the Socialist deputy, who had voluntarily re-enlisted. The Duke d'Ursel, the Catholic deputy, was in the uniform of the Guides; he wore crimson breeches and was close-shaven. One of the new Ministers, M. Emile Vandervelde, the Social-ist, was surrounded by a throng of people. They all turned and waved their handkerchiefs to the Queen.

The Princess, Prince Leopold and Prince Charles, dressed in black satin, were seated by their mother.

A confused sound of shouting came from the street. Four deputies and four senators left the House to meet the King. The usher announced:

"Gentlemen, the King."

He entered in military dress with gold epaulettes, his sword at his side, his kepi in his hand, and took his place in the centre, stripped off one of his white gloves, flung it into his képi, and gazed into the faces of two thousand Belgians, a heterogeneous and brilliant assembly—sena-tors, ministers, celebrities, journalists, officials and states-men, all on their feet, arms upraised, wildly proclaiming at the top of their voices their faith in him and their

love for him. He had never been calmer, more controlled, more sure of himself.

He spoke simply and slowly until he reached the passage: "When I look round on this profoundly-moved assembly which has only one thought . . ."

At these words the crowd went wild. Some of the Socialists wept. M. Woeste, who was very old, bent forward and made his hand into an ear-trumpet; ". . . to listen to the voice of Destiny."

". . . I ask you, gentlemen, have you irrevocably decided to preserve inviolate the sacred fatherland of our forebears?"

The whole House rose instantly to its feet. Only the two fair-haired little boys in their black satin suits remained seated by their mother, their eyes lifted and rivetted on their father's face.

The scene came to an end like a dream. . . . "I have faith in our destiny. Our country will not perish. God will be with us in our righteous cause. Long live Independent Belgium!"

When he had finished speaking, he quietly picked up his kepi, put on his white glove, and walked out, his sword clanking at his side. They heard him mount his horse, and it seemed as though the cheering crowd were bearing him on unseen shields. Hidden behind a curtain at one of the windows of the Legation, an Austrian diplomat was weeping. The royal procession disappeared.

CHAPTER VI

INVASION

O N August 5, 1914, a few people in the Rue de la Loi noticed a procession of cars leaving Brussels in the direction of Tervueren and Louvain. As the last one sped past, a secretary at the American Legation said to his chief: "The King."

He was right. The King was on his way to General Headquarters at Corbeek Loo near Louvain; he was to remain in the War zone for fifty-two months. In what condition would he find the precious human weapon with which he had been entrusted?

On the evening of August 7, M. de Broqueville had said: "Yes, but we have no heavy artillery. . . ." The Belgian army lacked far more than this. One hundred and eighty thousand men could be mobilized immediately, but they would be without officers and N.C.O.'s. Nor did they possess a single howitzer. There were only four hundred and two machine-guns. The King decided to defend Liége and Namur to the bitter end. Two divisions were sent to these positions. The other four were to hold the Gette, which was a three-day journey from Liége. The cavalry division was to be sent to the south.

The Belgian army had every moral qualification. It also had practically every technical disqualification. For many years the élite of the nation had ceased to send

their sons into the army. This was not only the case in the large industrial cities, where all that pertained to the army seemed, if not absurd, at any rate uninteresting and remote: the whole professional class, those who had best served the Belgian State for a hundred years, maintained an attitude of condescension and obstinate scepticism towards the army. In France the pick of the great schools had filled St. Cyr and the Polytechnique; in Belgium the majority of ecclesiastical teachers had been careful not to encourage the military vocation, even when they had not laid unction to their souls by conscientiously obliterating it from the hearts of their pupils.

For several years the Jesuits had actively striven against this persistent tendency, as if they guessed, like their French brethren, that they would one day give the lie to Renan's prophecy that the great German commander-in-chief would never be vanquished by one of their pupils. Père Lefèvre, a man of outstanding character and wide technical knowledge, had undertaken to lecture in the military schools. Many of the youthful captains and lieutenants of 1914 had emerged from his classes with flying colours. But this was an exception.

The cadre of the Belgian army, then, had been deprived of the best and most vital forces of the nation. Apart from a few scions of aristocracy, and a few Generals' sons, who had the army in their blood, it was composed almost entirely of brave and reliable men, who were often technically competent but lacked culture and understanding of human nature. Like all Belgians,

they were hard working, and showed the whole-hearted devotion to duty which is characteristic of the officer who has risen from the ranks. But they were totally ignorant of the conditions of European armies and the great problems of the day. In a country where the conservative officials declared that the army would never be called upon to fight, where the officers were told: "Be brave, be wise, be just . . . ," while they were informed in the same breath that they were an unnecessary luxury, it was only natural that a breach should have occurred between the nation and the army.

In the years that followed the War of 1870, the studies at the Ecole de Guerre had not been drawn up on any specified plan. There had been no uniformity. Only one man—a man head and shoulders above the rest—had managed to make order out of chaos. Major Galet was born "entre Sambre et Meuse." The son of a shoemaker, he had followed his father's trade, and had joined the army as a militiaman at the time when the nefarious system of drawing lots prevailed, the new recruit being the unlucky loser in the draw. It is touching to recall that the men of his village clubbed together to pay for his preparatory studies at the Military School; he entered it as a sergeant in the artillery in the same year as the King.

It has sometimes been said that it was there that a friendship sprang up between his royal fellow cadet and himself. As a matter of fact, Albert had been no more intimate with Galet at this period than with any other cadet in the School. When they left, their ways had diverged. Much later on, the future King, passing in

review the various branches of the Staff, had again encountered this demon for work, now a Staff Major and a lecturer at the Ecole de Guerre. Amongst many other attributes, Major Galet possessed that of lucidity. He was an excellent teacher, and his lectures were always to the point. "He makes everything as clear as daylight," said the King. From that day forth they were friends. The King appointed him his orderly officer, with the exceptional privilege of not being compelled to perform any purely decorative duty or attend any Court or society function. Major Galet had since lived a life of sober dignity, and his appointment was to give rise to a series of important events.

As if he wished to symbolize in himself all the virtues and defects of an army, the military confidant of the King had adopted the kind of life best calculated to set a wide distance between himself and both the man in the street and the common soldier. He had passed through the regulation stages in the various branches, had attained the rank of Staff Officer, and had donned the green uniform which destined its wearer to free himself thenceforth from all contact with the herd. He was a Protestant mystic and read his Bible devoutly; his voluntary conversion, extremely conspicuous in a country where secularity is the only rival to Catholicism, made him unique in Belgium. He lived the life of a hermit, always absorbed in his studies which were exclusively military; he never laughed—it seemed as if he had no time for laughter, and, the soul of integrity himself, he respected the convictions of others.

Major Galet was as high-minded as his Sovereign. Nevertheless, he was to be the cause of bitter discord in the General Staff. In addition, he countenanced a certain amount of favouritism amongst the generals and did not rid the army of other leaders who had grown old in the bureaucracy of peace-time and were totally unfit to cope with the catastrophic situation with which they were faced during the first months of the War. The same thing applied to many of the French generals; and the mournful procession was to join them after two months' fighting at Limoges, the rendez-vous of failures. With the exception of General Drubbel, General Michel, and General de Witte, no 1914 Belgian officer was to retain his position of command at the end of the War.

This was all the more tragic in view of the fact that the leaders, hopelessly incompetent as they were, showed real devotion to their country. During the first weeks of the War, young would-be volunteers had besieged the recruiting offices, begging to be allowed to fight, but there were neither arms nor equipment, nor indeed any officers to lead them. The battalions consisted of mo-bilized men, of whom many had served their time as "mercenaries"—those who acted as substitutes for their contemporaries who were in a position to buy them-selves off. This disgraceful system exposed the amazing shortsightedness of those in power. Meanwhile, stu-dents from the universities and men from every walk of life hastened to join up, and it is impossible to say which was the more regrettable: their inability to use a rifle or a small scale map, or the want of appreciation

shown by those in authority in taking advantage of their heroic eagerness to serve.

The attack on Liége was the attack on a symbol. The system of defence by means of fortified positions had at least the ironic advantage of making each attacked city a martyr city. For many centuries, the town and principality of Liége had had an intensely individual life of its own. It had developed the regional spirit more than any other province. The vernacular and the language of the theatre was a particularly racy brand of Walloon. The people of Liége, fervently Liégeois, claimed to be the most distinguished, the most advanced, the most musical and the most Gallicized of all the Belgians. Proud of their ecclesiastical traditions, they none the less believed themselves to be the most daring freethinkers. They had, of course, been certain that on the plateau of Hervé, Landen and Herstal, the cradle of the great Carolingians, the war between Germany and Latinity would be decided. And they were not very far wrong. While Namur, after a gallant resistance under the splendid leadership of General Michel, was to see its troops fall back on France, Liége bore the first shock of the invasion, that of the covering army corps which had been on the march since August 4, before the German mobilization was completed.

Under the command of General Leman, Liége was held by thirty-two thousand infantry, five hundred lancers, one hundred and fifty guns and thirty machineguns. On August 4, at about eight o'clock in the morning, five German columns, coming from Eupen, Mal-

médy and Aix-la-Chapelle, advanced on Liége, by the
five routes of Gemmenich, Henri-Chapelle, Limbourg,
Spa and Stavelot. They numbered thirty-five thousand
infantry, fourteen thousand cavalry, one hundred machine-guns and one hundred guns, including eight two
hundred and ten trench mortars, a squadron of planes
and a Zeppelin. These figures speak for themselves—
they are eloquent of haste. This heavily equipped mass
advanced in perfect order on a thirty-mile front. During the night, the infantry was to steal between the
forts. The Uhlans, crossing the Meuse to the north and
south of the front, were to overrun the country at the
same time and terrorize the inhabitants. Forty-eight
hours had been allowed for this operation.

At one o'clock in the afternoon the cavalry from the
north appeared on the banks of the Meuse, at the point
where it was nearest to German territory. At Visé,
their scouts were hastening forward to cross the bridge,
when they saw that it had been destroyed. On the left
bank a battalion of the 12th Belgian Division opened
heavy fire on them. The cavalry, without pontoon
troops (the Belgian peasants had felled the trees and
blocked the road), without infantry (which spent the
day in clearing away the fallen trunks), managed to cross
the river six hundred yards from the Dutch frontier.
But that was all. At five o'clock that afternoon the
Belgian battalion ceased fire. On the opposite bank
the Germans, foiled in their attack, halted. To the
south the German columns had pursued their encir-
cling movement. Night fell. Thus ended the first day

of the War in Belgium.   Fair progress in the south.   A bloody check in the north.

On August 5, at ten A.M., a battalion of the 27th German Brigade reached the foot of the slope on which stood the Fortress of Barchon.   The great struggle had begun.

It started with a day of delay for the Germans.   On the fourth, and not until the fourth, the King had at length agreed, in the face of the actual violation of Belgian territory, to ask the help of those who were to become his allies.   The following note was despatched to the Governments of Great Britain, France and Russia:

"The Belgian Government regrets to announce that this morning German forces crossed into Belgian territory, thereby violating the guarantees given under the Treaty.   The Government of the King is firmly resolved to hold out by every means in its power.   Belgium appeals to England, France and Russia to co-operate as guarantors in the defence of her territory. There must be concerted and mutual action, having as its aim resistance to the force used by Germany against Belgium, and at the same time, the guaranteeing of the maintenance of Belgium's independence and her future integrity.   Belgium is happy to be able to state that she will ensure the defence of her key positions."

Before the Allies could put their plans into action, Germany gave unmistakable signs of her intentions by the attack on Liége.   They may be defined in one word: brigandage.   The frontier had been violated before the completion of diplomatic formalities.   Outside the walls of the fortress, those German officers who were most

resolved to push through, regardless of all the rules of war, were to win most favour in the eyes of their superiors. Within the walls, it was a spy who earned the greatest distinction. Captain Brinkman, the German Military Attaché in Brussels, whom the Belgian Government had been unwise enough not to keep under surveillance, went to General Leman's headquarters in the Rue Sainte Foi in the heart of Liége, at about nine o'clock on August 5. He stated that he had been sent on a mission to the General; that, nothwithstanding the German Ultimatum and the Belgian reply, negotiations were still going on between the two Governments; and that it was "in the interests of the Belgian army not to commit any acts of hostility for the time being. . . ."

Captain Brinkman said further that he had decided to wait for the reply of the King's Government until one P.M.: "After that hour, and unless a satisfactory reply is received, the town of Liége will be bombed by Zeppelins."

The interview came to an end almost at the very moment when the 27th Brigade was ordered to attack. Fighting continued the whole afternoon, increasing in violence. Towards evening the King, whose suspicions were aroused, telephoned to General Leman that there might be a fresh surprise attack and impressed on him that he must therefore protect his headquarters. Simultaneously, the 7th and 10th Army Corps attacked. Six Brigades advanced on a twenty-two-mile front. Only one got through. Its Commander was killed. It wavered under fire from the Fortress of Fléron and seemed about to give way when the Quartermaster-General of

the 2nd Army, General Ludendorff, appeared. From the third day of the War, this man revealed the full extent of his power. He re-formed the Army Corps, led it to a position between Fléron and Evegnié at midnight, and succeeded in mustering it on the plateau of Belle Flamme, below Liége.

This, the only one of six attempts to succeed, was nevertheless a military triumph. But the Germans, seemingly, wanted a spectacular display of brigandage. At four-thirty A.M. light infantry in grey-green caps stole between the fortresses of Pontisse and La Meuse, and penetrated into the outskirts of Liége. The inhabitants, who saw them pass, mistook them for English troops. With their handkerchiefs and white gloves, the five officers and fifty men walked along the Rue Sainte Foi, and were only recognized by the Staff at Headquarters. There, in the very heart of the defence, they fought with revolvers. General Leman had only just time to escape to the Fortress of Loncin. The advice of the King had been disregarded. For two hours the telephone between the King's Headquarters and those at Liége was silent. At Louvain the people were terror-stricken. At length telephonic communication was restored, and the King was able to grasp the full gravity of the situation.

Alone, in the breach made at Fléron, Ludendorff and his Brigade were wondering where their heroic audacity would lead them. "After we had penetrated Fléron, our situation was exceedingly serious," wrote Ludendorff. "No information reached us from the other Brigades. . . ." The position had been firmly held, but

it was useless for the 3rd Belgian Division to let itself
be massacred by four German Army Corps. An order
came from Louvain for it to rejoin the bulk of the Belgian army at the Gette. On August 7, Leman shut
himself up in Loncin and resolved that he would let
the fortress with its twelve cupolas be blown sky-high
rather than yield. On the same day the King telephoned to Joffre: "The Fortress has been ordered to
hold out until the end"; and to the Burgomaster of
Liége he sent this message: "We must defend our territory, even at the cost of our cities."

Belgium had found a man who spoke in her name.
The voice of the Leader rang out across her frontiers,
charged with the will of a King resolved never to yield.
The glorious tidings of honour and heroïsm went forth
to dumbfounded Berlin, to wildly enthusiastic Paris and
London, to the most distant capitals of the old world
and the new. Simple words, but spoken with such dignity that the fame of the King spread like wild-fire
round the globe.

At six P.M. on August 12, the first sixteen-inch shells
burst on the fortress of Barchon. For four days the
gigantic guns spewed forth their leaden masses. On
the sixteenth all was over. The Fortress of Loncin had
been blown to bits. Leman was discovered unconscious
amidst the ruins. Thus ended the resistance of Liége.

Notwithstanding "brigandage" and the Ludendorff
coup, the German operation of "forty-eight" hours had
lasted twelve days. It was more than the Allied armies
had dared to hope. Liége was decorated by the Legion

of Honour.   From being a symbol, the mission of the
old Lotharingian town had become a reality.   The entire country thrilled with ardent hope.   The King's
proclamation of August 8 was repeated on all sides:
"Men, you are the advance-guard of the great armies
engaged in this gigantic struggle. . . ."   Who could
have foreseen that even greater armies would soon ren-
der the struggle even more gigantic?   Who could have
prophesied how far Belgium's long cortège of death and
agony would stretch, driven on before the thundering
wave of the German offensive?   One thing was certain:
the French army, deflected by Plan 17 and concentrated
in the East, would never re-join the general advance
guard formed by the Belgian army.

Whilst the garrison troops of Liége, utterly exhausted, were retreating through the country they had
so gloriously defended, and had fallen back on the
Gette, another victory, that of Haelen, brought comfort to the heart of the King's army.   At Haelen the
advance guards of both sides were able to show all their
quality in a single encounter.   There the heroism of
the Belgian soldiers was made plain to all eyes, and
although no great number of troops was involved, the
memory of this cavalry skirmish remained an undying
one in both camps.

The Belgian cavalry of 1914, like the French, were
the only soldiers who still wore resplendent, picturesque
and cumbersome uniforms.   The inhabitants of the big
cities had only seen them in full dress, with aigrettes
and plumes, their parade and review uniform.   Their

entire accoutrement was reminiscent of the past. The tight, frogged dolman had been replaced by a tunic, and the officers had substituted gold stripes on their cuffs for stars on their collars. But all four regiments of Chasseurs retained the shako, the Lancers the *shapka,* and the Guides the busby. Four cavalry regiments formed a division, whose equipment was so out of date that its one machine-gun section was notorious throughout the army. At General Headquarters, this section was called by the name of its commanding officer, Ouverleaux. The division was under the command of Lieutenant-General de Witte, a cavalry officer of the traditional type, a leader rather than a tactician, but confident of himself and his men, a soldier to the core, imbued with the spirit of offensive.

At Haelen the cavalry still wore their elegant headgear. The Germans, armed with lances, were equipped according to modern ideas. The Hussars retained their frogged tunics, as did those famous Death's Head Hussars, in whose ranks the members of the Berlin Herrenclub were anxious to win their stripes as officers of the Reserve. So great was the prestige of these glorious units that the great statesmen of the Reich always wore their uniform on ceremonial occasions. There was a certain Captain von der Lancken on the Reserve of the Uhlans of the Guard, of whom more will be said later. Many of the great men of the Empire had served in these regiments, amongst them Von Schlieffen, and Von Mackensen who, at the zenith of his military glory, remained faithful to the uniform of the Death's Head Hussars. This fine regiment must have had the spirit

of attack in its very blood to have accompanied the
Uhlans in their break-neck raids. At their head the
most illustrious names were to be found; amongst them,
curiously enough, the ancient names of Huguenot émi-
grés, such as Le Tanneur de St. Paul (Horse Artillery)
and Digeon de Monteton.

Such were the adversaries that the Belgian troops encountered on the morning of August 12, 1914, at
Haelen, southwest of Diest, that sandy and mystic region where monasteries and convents abound. There
is no more calm and peaceful spot than Diest, at that
time enclosed within its walls as though Vauban might
return on the morrow to lay siege to it. In the lovely
region of the Campine, the peasants are the most independent and peace-loving in the world. From the
risings against the Convention down to the Catholic
manifestations in 1912, we find their ancient dictum:
niemand gedwangen soldaat—no man is obliged to be a
soldier. Yet it was on these very meadows, between
the Gette and the Dyle, that the Belgian soldiers, most
of them of peasant stock, were to inflict a humiliating
check on Germany's proudest and most warlike regiments.

The King's order ran: "There is reason to believe
that a German cavalry attack is about to take place at
St. Trond, in the neighbourhood of Hasselt, and subsequently to the north of Diest. The duty of the cavalry
division is to cover the left flank of the army. The
vicinity of Diest may become increasingly dangerous."
On August 9, in fact, the Death's Head Hussars entered
St. Trond, and an entire division followed them in the

direction of Louvain. On the eleventh, these regiments were still on the move. On the twelfth, at eight o'clock in the morning, a detachment of Lancers in field-grey galloped up to the bridge of Haelen. The Belgian Lancers, concealed as snipers, shot them down. It was a good beginning.

General de Witte had under his command the 1st and 2nd regiments of Guides, the 4th and 5th Lancers, a body of horse-artillery, a company of armed cyclists, and the 4th and 24th regiments of the line. He wisely used all the men of the cavalry regiments as sharp-shooters. At about half-past eight the German attacks began. Crouching down in the undergrowth, deter-mined to die rather than yield an inch, the Belgian sol-diers behaved with extraordinary coolness. General von der Marwitz grew impatient and gave his cavalry the order to charge. The Mecklenburg Dragoons, Lancers, Uhlans—four regiments were literally mowed down. Under the blazing sun the Belgian troops kept their heads like hardened campaigners, and continued firing from nine o'clock in the morning till six at night.

The flower of the German cavalry fell on this battle-field. The bloody engagement, which may be likened to Waterloo and the British squares, filled the Belgians with legitimate pride. The story of the epic encounter spread throughout the army, and also, no doubt, throughout the German ranks, for, from that day forth, the Kaiser's cavalry displayed extraordinary discretion both in its advance towards Paris and towards the coast. In the *French Cavalry Review* (May-June, 1920), Major Prioux, attached to the French G.H.Q. at the beginning

of the War, made the following comment on this sudden slowing-down:

"After a survey of the battle of August 12, 1914, we may ask ourselves whether the leaders of the German cavalry, when they had subsequently to order their divisions to attack, were not haunted at times by the memory of the splendid squadrons who fell in bloody heaps on the road from Haelen to Iserbeek."

On that same night of August 12, the heavy guns began to bombard the cupolas of Liége; but on the road from Haelen to Hasselt, riderless horses of dragoons and lancers galloped madly along, unheeding the desperate calls of the bugles. . . .

Far more than an advance guard was needed to defeat the Belgians. It would need the entire colossal German army.

What secret hope did the Kaiser's General Staff cherish at the beginning of August? Perhaps they thought that the Belgian Government, once it had made the gesture for which its word of honour had called, would stop at that and, having done its moral duty, would leave to the Allies the task of defending the territory whose protection they had guaranteed. On two occasions, propositions to this effect were made. How little Germany knew the King and his Ministers!

Did the Germans also believe that the Belgian army would be swept away like chaff on the wind? They had certainly believed that Liége would fall instantly before a sudden offensive, and that the retreat of the King to Antwerp was a mere formality that could be

disregarded. They were to be deeply disillusioned. The rôle of Belgium had a dual significance: spiritual and material. From the Gette to the Marne, all along the immense zone invaded by the Schlieffen Plan, it continually made itself felt.

The Schlieffen Plan had been known to exist beyond doubt, and so many confirmatory reports had been received in diplomatic circles that it seemed as though the French G.H.Q. would base their line of action on its structure. The German plans, which were accessible to all the initiated, were specific. As for the enormous extension of German railroads through the sparsely inhabited forests of the Eiffel, any motor-cyclist could have gauged their length, any officer could have seen that these lines were not intended for peace-time traffic. Belgium would once again become the classic scene of invasion.

The only man who had obstinately refused to realize this was the French Generalissimo. Joffre, with that mulish and taciturn obstinacy which was innate in his character, turned his entire army towards the east, Maubeuge being his furthest position westward. This was the famous Plan 17, feasible enough on paper, but the consequences of which were to prove unspeakably disastrous to Belgium. The most that can be said for Plan 17 is that when it was revealed to an international tribunal, it disproved the absurd German accusation that the French had been prepared for a "defensive offensive" across Belgium. They were, as a matter of fact, so little prepared that their defensive was ex-

tremely weak, all their strength being concentrated on the east.

The Germans worked out the situation with devastating logic. Von Kluck and von Bülow, when they crossed the Meuse at Liége, knew exactly where they were going. Joffre needed at least a fortnight to move his armies towards the west. General Lanrezac, with a foresight that cost him his command, had prophesied this situation from the beginning. When Joffre, on Lanrezac's left wing, urged him to attack on the north of the Sambre, between Thuin and Namur, he refused point-blank, realizing how disastrous such an attack would be. Lanrezac, for whom King Albert professed a warm admiration, retreated in accordance with the rules of the Belgian G.H.Q. His character, his pessimistic and hypercritical mind, so like Major Galet's, disposed him towards these rules. His disagreement with Joffre led to a definite break.

Each point in the German programme was carried out, as though their movements were regulated by a stop-watch adjusted to a hair. Those troops which had been ordered by von Emmich to attack Liége were covering troops. Joffre obstinately insisted that the entire German offensive would be carried out by their regulars. He would not bother his head about their reserves, believing them to be unfitted for an attack of such magnitude. But though the German mobilization had only been in progress for three days on August 4, on the twelfth it had reached such a point that regiments consisting of reservists, who had come from the

furthest frontiers of the empire, were swarming over Belgian territory in grey masses.

Joffre had underestimated the number of his enemies by fifty per cent. Not until the frontier battle was he to realize his mistake. When the Belgian army on the Gette made their first retreating movement, Colonel Aldebert, a French attaché, who had brought despatches from the French G.H.Q., exclaimed: "Good Heavens, you are retreating before a mere cavalry screen!" This "mere cavalry screen" was twelve army corps.

On August 17, the terrible tidings reached Louvain. On the eighteenth, more catastrophic news had been received. It was learnt that the last fortresses of Liége had fallen, that General Leman was a prisoner, and that German regiments had crossed the Meuse on three pontoons at Huy from east to west. The enveloping movement had reached colossal dimensions. Implacably, the despatches continued to arrive, each as categoric as its predecessor. On August 9, the King had informed the French and British G.H.Q.s that if any very large force appeared to the north of the Meuse, he thought he would be obliged to avoid the massacre of the entire Belgian army by withdrawing temporarily on Antwerp, with the intention of resuming the offensive as soon as the Allied armies were known to be in the vicinity. The King had withdrawn to Malines, where he was staying in the château of Battel. For the last time, as the enemy came on, he ascended the tower of the Hôtel de Ville, gazed through his field-glasses at the country-side, then rushed up and down the stairs with such

break-neck strides that his orderlies sweated great drops beneath their busbies. In such anxious moments as these, he would feel the need to expend some of his prodigious physical energy.

The enemy waves surged across the Hesbaye with appalling regularity. This is the most fertile region of Belgium, the home of the most prosperous peasants. The troops fired the villages as they marched through, and von Kluck answered each resistance of the Belgian army by terrorizing the civil population. On August 19, it was plain that all hope of joining the Allied armies would have to be abandoned. The Hesbaye, from Hasselt to Huy, shook with the trampling feet of half a million men. On that morning, at about five o'clock, the advance guard of the 4th German Army Corps reached Louvain. Another attacked Aerschot. These two names have a sinister ring in the memory of Belgians.

This first part of the campaign was the more dreadful because the German troops deliberately went out of their way to vent on the civil population their fury at the disastrous check they had received. Mass hypnotism must have been rigorously exercised over the German army for the troops to have believed so easily in the legend of the sharp-shooters. Not a single German soldier was ever able to assert to a Committee of Enquiry that he had caught a Belgian civilian *in flagrante delictu*. On the contrary, officers who had gone out to reconnoitre admitted on their return that they had been unable to discover any culprit.

There is nothing more likely than that cases of irreg-

ular conduct may have occurred in an overpopulated country like Belgium. It would not have been so very extraordinary if an excited civilian had fired on a German advance guard. But even if it were true, it would hardly be a justification for the vindictiveness of the German officers. It will never explain why byres full of cattle and granaries stocked with wheat were burnt at Bastogne, nor why five thousand civilians, men, women and children, were summarily shot at Namur, Liége, Tournai and Malines.

Long, long afterwards, in 1926, Gustav Stresemann told Fernand Neuray, the Belgian journalist, in confidence: "The invasion of Belgium in 1914 was a blunder; the legend we spread about sharp-shooters, and the cruelties committed by our troops were an even worse blunder."

The Belgians made their first resistance at Visé. The four thousand inhabitants of the town were driven out, and the whole place, down to the very apple trees in the orchards, was set alight. Look at the map of Belgium. From Visé to Malines, we can trace a scarlet line. The myth, the eternal excuse put forward, was that of sharp-shooters, and it was so well backed up that Belgian investigators found letters to German soldiers from their parents, imploring them to be on the watch against the vile Belgian peasants. The Kaiser, sincerely or otherwise, addressed a protest to President Wilson from Louvain, in which he said: "My heart bleeds."

Perhaps, although it has never been proven, the Germans really believed that the Belgium of 1914 would be the theatre of guerilla warfare similar to that of

Napoleon's Spanish campaign—a peasantry raised by *alcaldes* and priests. At any rate, it is certain that the first buildings to be shelled were the churches, the first civilians to be shot were the curés, the first to be ill-treated were the burgomasters. The whole civilized world was aghast.

The King and Queen heard these tidings at Antwerp, whither they had been forced to retire. In the Place de Meir, when Albert and Elisabeth strolled through the gardens on those hot nights, the wind from the east wafted the acrid breath of the flames to them.

The army, in retreat on Antwerp, had left open the road to Brussels. Up till August 20, the vast majority of Belgians still believed the fortresses of Liége to be impregnable. General Leman had been a prisoner for four days; but it now became plain that in modern warfare a vast number of people could be kept in entire ignorance of their approaching fate. Only the news of the massacres was spread, for nothing is so contagious as terror. "Liége is still holding out," they said, "so how can the enemy troops reach Brussels?" At two-thirty P.M., however, the General in command of the 4th German Army Corps entered the capital. Burgomaster Max received him, standing stiffly erect, and refused to shake hands.

Like Vienna in 1805, Brussels gave in without a struggle. Three Prussian officers went to the Hôtel de Ville. While they were engaged in discussion the German troops marched through the Rue de la Loi to the sound of fifes. It was a strange scene. The people of

Brussels had no notion of the German conception of manly good looks, nor of the physiognomy of the German soldier. It was extremely hot. The cobblestones were slippery. Idlers, shopkeepers and students roamed through the desolate streets. The 4th Army Corps passed by in icy silence. The weary infantry dragged itself along; the tail end of the columns could scarcely keep up. At three o'clock the band turned the corner of the Rue de la Colline, and streamed into the Grand' Place.

Not since 1815 had a foreign army filed past those great façades. The Grand' Place of Brussels, with its gilded houses, its gables, the dream-like lacework of its spires and turrets, looks like a gigantic plaything, a fairy-tale creation sprung from the imagination of a Burgundian *jongleur*. It is surrounded by a labyrinth of alleys and *culs-de-sac*, an incredibly tangled web of passages crowded with shops and restaurants. The German troops entered the Grand' Place on one side and goose-stepped across. The drums rolled continuously. The fife-players were out of breath. The pennon of Brussels still hung from the spire of the Hôtel de Ville, the Belgian flag still waved over its doors. An officer's horse fell with a screech of slipping iron. The Uhlans' mounts could not keep their footing on the cobbles, but stumbled like unpractised dancers. The fifes began to play again.

That night, the Grand' Place was jammed. The Germans had established their headquarters at the Hôtel de Ville, and had ordered beds to be set up in the great Gothic hall. It was a strange metamorphosis: a historic

building, a storehouse of treasures, had become a barracks. Soldiers in their thousands were sitting on their kit-bags. Many seemed to be utterly exhausted. The bugles marked the hours, and brought back the memory of the ritual of the past in the setting that had come down from Philip the Good—the setting in which Reinhardt had often yearned to produce magnificent pageants.

The endless files of men marched noisily down the wide Rue du Cinquantenaire to the Rue Royale—staff officers, battalions, artillery, travelling kitchens, gun-carriages loaded with provisions, including whole sheep and pigs, whose bloody carcases swayed to and fro. Whenever a soldier went into an *estaminet*, dozens of small boys glued their faces to the window to watch him drink his glass of beer. This went on for two days. The crowd was gloomy, restless and sarcastic. They expected portentous events, were amazed that there was neither firing nor bloodshed, and that a capital could be occupied with so little disturbance. Four days later the news that the fortresses of Liége had been blown up spread from lip to lip. And the captivity began.

The Belgians noted with surprise that the German officers were either squat and red-faced, or tall and lean, with scarred faces, and monocles stuck in their eyes. Squadrons of hussars galloped into the precincts of St. Gudule, singing noisily. Next came the munition wagons, a stream of lorries, and an entire train of pontoons reversed on gun-carriages, their bottoms plastered with mud from the Meuse. The city was put under

the orders of Major-General von Jarotsky, commander
of the 16th infantry brigade.

On August 26, the Imperial Cabinet appointed Field
Marshal von der Goltz as Governor-General of all the
occupied territory of Belgium. Dr. von Sandt was appointed Civil Administrator. On September 2, a Proclamation, signed by the Field-Marshal, set forth the
various regulations. Amongst these, it was stated that:
"The Governor requires no one to renounce his patriotic feelings." This, however, did not prevent him
from levying an immediate contribution of fifty million
francs on the city. M. Max, the Burgomaster, replied
that the treasury had been transferred to Antwerp,
which was true, but which met with the unexpected
retort from Jarotsky: "That's a lie." Meanwhile the invaders dared not as yet order the inhabitants to take
down their flags. In the great salons of the King's
Palace, which had been converted into wards, two tiny
Belgian flags had been pinned over every bed. A month
earlier the Queen had pointed them out to Brand
Whitlock, with the words: "The children put them
there. . . ." The children were Charles-Theodore,
Count of Flanders, and Leopold, Duke of Brabant.

CHAPTER VII

RETREAT

DAY by day the breach separating Brussels and Antwerp grew a little wider. The only definite news that came through during those days of uncertainty were the tidings of the horrors at Tamines, Aerschot and Visé. Hugh Gibson, Secretary at the American Legation, had managed to get through the lines and travel across the country. Those in the know were aware that the German armies had met with a check on the Marne. Major-General von Luttwitz, Jarotsky's successor, explained to the Spanish Ambassador, the Marquis de Villalobar, that it was no longer a question of taking Paris but of capturing the entire French army with a single sweep of the net. As he spoke, he sketched a wide circle in the air. This was the man who said to Brand Whitlock on August 26: "A terrible thing has happened at Louvain. The general in command of the city was talking to the burgomaster when the burgomaster's son shot him dead, and the population began firing on the German troops. . . ."

On August 19, however, the Germans had reached only as far as Namur. They themselves realized that it would take one hundred and twenty thousand men and four hundred howitzers to attack this new position. One sixth of the Belgian army had concentrated there, expecting to be reinforced by the French advance guard.

But of the latter, only Mangin's Brigade got as far as
Dinant. The fifteen thousand defensive troops of
Namur who had withdrawn in time when the heavy
guns had begun their work, reached Rouen, and, going
via Le Havre, rejoined their comrades at Antwerp.

The part played by the King was temporarily limited
to defending the northwest and the west of Belgium,
and to hindering the German troops on their march to
France by making sorties. In pursuance of this plan,
two sorties were carried out; on August 25 and September 2, the Belgian troops thrust desperately forward
near Aerschot and Malines. With its eighty thousand
men, the Belgian army was thus able to divert ten thousand marines, who had already reached Brussels and
were on their way to Paris; it also abruptly deflected towards the north twenty thousand infantry, forty thousand men of the 9th Army Corps, the 3rd Reserve Corps,
the mixed brigade of the 15th, and seven or eight brigades of Landwehr and Ersatz. These German forces
numbered one hundred and fifty thousand men in all.
In addition, the destruction of the railroad on the
Liége-Brussels-Mons line prevented the convoy of troops
from Strasbourg to St. Quentin; and so much confusion
was caused that, according to the invaders themselves,
its repercussions were felt in the very heart of Germany.
This was the Belgian contribution to the Battle of the
Marne.

The story of Antwerp is nevertheless one of disappointment. Obsessed by its old idea of a national refuge, the Belgian Staff had abandoned the greater part
of the country and had shut itself in. Within this cir-

cle, some asserted that Antwerp was impregnable and that no army could ever take it. Others maintained the contrary, and disputes grew more and more vociferous amongst the members of the War Tribunal.

The King was compelled to intervene, and by his personal action averted a crisis in the Staff. Ever since Louvain—ever since 1913, in fact—trouble had been brewing. General de Selliers de Moranville had been appointed Chief of Staff on the recommendation of M. de Broqueville. Through Major Galet, General de Ryckel had been appointed Second in Command against the wishes of General de Selliers. Thus there were two factions, actually two commands, in constant conflict. General de Ryckel, a shrewd, suspicious and cautious soldier, who had been entrusted in 1913 with the drawing up of a plan of campaign, had lost himself in conjecture and produced nothing. At Louvain the Ryckel clique, which was in favour of a defence on the Meuse, was openly at variance with the Selliers clan.

Meanwhile, like an enigmatic personification of wisdom, Major Galet in his green uniform leant silently and thoughtfully against the mantelpiece, listening closely and preparing expert reports. The King, whose natural inclination was to compare all theories and examine them in their various aspects, scrutinized and re-scrutinized them. His mind, so resolute in the face of danger, his heart, so valiant when there was duty to be done, wavered in this battle of opinions where it seemed to him that the award should go to the ablest, not to the bravest.

Finally, General de Selliers was despatched to France

and General de Ryckel to Russia. Colonel Wielemans, Head of the Ministerial Department, was abruptly promoted to the position of Chief of Staff; and as his military rank was not in keeping with his appointment, the King regularized matters by associating with him his old tutor Jungbluth, who, if he did not possess the necessary qualifications, did at least possess the necessary rank. But Colonel Wielemans was the controlling brain. This coup of M. de Broqueville's in arbitrarily nominating the military leader of his choice by a stroke of political daring was very much *à la* Clémenceau.

The King was perfectly cool and self-controlled. Jules Destrée, who was trying, in company with other great writers, to do some work for the cause, was received by him at this time. The Socialist orator was struck by the dignified cordiality of the King, his lack of agitation, and his quick grasp of a situation. He read as much then as in peacetime, and his thoughts still oscillated between distant lands where the glory of Belgium was but half known, and the trenches, so near to the precincts of Antwerp.

Those days in Antwerp might be called the blackest days of all. Liége had been heroic revelation: Antwerp was racking anxiety. The two sorties had had a shattering effect on the morale of the German army; but during their heroic raids on the enemy lines the Belgian soldiers had passed through sacked villages, burnt towns. Thousands of Belgians had left their homes and had taken with them what they could on any kind of vehicle they could get. As they went through

the villages, driving the grey hordes before them, the Belgian soldiers had seen through the open doors of houses whole families, fathers, mothers and children, seated round the tables, dead. . . .

The Government had rejoined the King at Antwerp. The city was cluttered up by well-meaning politicians, and the national refuge had become a refuge indeed in the full meaning of the word. Hugh Gibson, who was now the United States Ambassador, saw the King during this period near Malines while one of the sorties was in progress. He was standing in a turnip field, gazing through his field-glasses. His black uniform was spattered with the mud of the battlefields. Here he appeared in all his grandeur, whereas, in his apartments in the Place de Meir in the very heart of the city, he could not breathe. Intrigues and polemics were utterly foreign to his nature. Old M. Woeste, despatched as negotiator to the King's defending army by von der Goltz, reached Antwerp from Brussels. But he never succeeded in reaching the King's study.

It was the King who had managed to communicate with the authorities in Brussels and insist that no armed resistance should be made at the gates of the capital. A few civic guards had conceived the untimely idea of overturning trams on the road from Louvain—a pitifully obvious procedure. The old tradition of barricade warfare was a myth to which these good people clung tenaciously; their ignorance was touching, their absurdity almost sublime. There could be no question of barricades before von Kluck and von Bülow.

Once more, then, the King was able to avert the sac-

rifice of numbers of lives. In Antwerp, excited groups, described by Fernand Neuray as "honourable conspiracies," held heated discussions and swung from the most unfounded optimism to the blackest pessimism. At Liége and Louvain all had been warlike. At the Yser everything was to be heroic. Liége and the Yser were to be epochs. Antwerp was no more than an episode. It was fortunate that there, too, the supreme decisions were entrusted to a man who, even in the merest trifles, swiftly and deliberately shook himself free of conventional trammels.

There was something profoundly moving about the arrival of the Queen and Princes at Folkestone. A mailboat had already brought over the royal luggage. Lord Curzon, whose friendship with the Belgian royal family was of long standing, had offered them his house, and they had instantly accepted his hospitality. The Queen crossed on one day and returned the next. Like a true soldier, once she had left her children in safety, she went back to Antwerp.

How often has England opened her doors to royal fugitives! All such arrivals have an atmosphere of melancholy. But in this case the royal family had not been driven into exile by their people. Even less was it the act of a dynasty abandoning its country through misfortune. But pessimists asked anxiously if this were not the beginning of the end—and what an end! Would suffering, heroically borne, be their only crown? No one could foresee the whole story, or that the hour

would come when all their agony would be repaid a hundredfold.

Prince Leopold had been entered at Eton. Prince Charles was to be a naval cadet. Princess Marie-José was to continue, in Italy, the studies she had already seriously begun there.

On the morning of October 4, two thousand English sailors, brought over by Winston Churchill, arrived in Antwerp. Amongst my childhood memories, I shall never forget having seen the First Lord of the Admiralty driving through Bruges in his car, with his wing collar and his big cigar. The Naval Brigade was a heterogeneous collection of men, hastily got together from every sphere of life. Rifles and cartridges had been hurriedly served out to them, and all were fully resolved to uphold the honour of the Union Jack. The crowd gave them a wild ovation.

But what aberration of his fertile brain had made Winston believe he could defend a city whose spires were of no stronger material than those of Liége and Namur? At a time when the Germans were attacking Lille and penetrating Flanders, this time to the south, Antwerp ran the risk of being completely cut off from the rest of the world and of undergoing the fate of Metz, in which case the King and Churchill himself would have been imprisoned like Bazaine.

At Lierre, the charming little town of artists and nuns, King George's sailors fought their first engagement. Nearly a hundred years ago their ancestors had won glory on the soil of Flanders. But we must turn

back the pages of history a further hundred years before
Wellington to find still other English soldiers doing
battle on Belgian territory—to the victories of that other
Churchill, the great Duke of Marlborough, the Churchill of Blenheim and Malplaquet. Had this memory
haunted the dreams of the First Lord of the Admiralty?

England had been slow to intervene on behalf of
Belgium. Her armies were sent to the relief of a position whose defence was already a myth. On October 3,
Sir Edward Grey wired that eight thousand men with
heavy artillery had left for the front, and that eighteen
thousand would follow. It was more than time. On
the previous night the King had sent a message that
Ghent was in danger. At Ostend, opposite Fort Wellington, which had been turned into a race-course, the
first British troop-ships came into sight. On a foggy
autumn evening the first Scottish regiments filed
through Bruges. The pipers marched beneath the
Porte Maréchal, the western gate, with their swinging
step, and the plaintive wail of the bagpipes rose up to
the high Spanish gables and echoed on the ramparts.
The crowd went wild with enthusiasm over the brave
show made by the kilted giants, the perfect rhythm of
their movements, and the inmaculate turn-out of General Rawlinson's escort.

At last, Belgians and British were going to meet.
The French, too, aware of the danger threatening the
lines round Ghent, despatched a Brigade of Naval
Marines under Admiral Ronarch. On the sixth, however, the Germans threatened Termonde. One by one

the Belgian regiments crossed the Scheldt from east to west, and the exodus began.

I have found a touching reminder of those last perilous hours at Antwerp—two photographs of Albert and Elisabeth in the courtyard of their Palace. The first one shows them full face, the second is a back view. As usual the King has his hands behind him; he has to stoop to talk to the Queen, and his expression is unspeakably troubled, as if he alone were bearing on his shoulders the weight of the sorrows and disasters of Belgium. The Queen looks anxious but undaunted. Is he giving her advice, or is she encouraging him? Those who saw them thus in their courtyard during the last moments at Antwerp, when the quartermaster-sergeants were loading up the lorries, must have felt that they were not treading the flat stones but climbing to still greater glory.

The retreat was a terrifying business. From the mouth of the Scheldt to that of the Yser, Flanders is flat and marshy. To the west of Antwerp lies the country of Waes; a succession of meadows and rectangular fields surrounded by poplars and willows; a terrain so damp that on the finest days the sun is shrouded in an opaque white veil. It is a brooding, restless, and over-populated region, where village encroaches on village. From Antwerp clear to Ghent the road is one long street, lined with houses all exactly alike, which swarm with children.

Refugees from all these hamlets followed the troops in indescribable chaos and confusion. No other retreat

can give any idea of this retreat, because it took place
across the most populous country in the world. Am-
munition lorries and gun-carriages conveyed women,
children, old men and the most extraordinary parapher-
nalia; the procession resembled a long trail of caravans
accompanied by the clamour heard in Arab bazaars, a
mixture of oaths, wails, the shouting of men, the bellow-
ing of cattle and the clucking of hens. The wounded
were given priority in the waggons. The horses, that
were not to be unharnessed for twenty days, jogged on
mechanically, with drooping heads. An officer met two
well-dressed girls supporting their octogenarian father.
He gave the old man a seat on a gun-carriage. An hour
later the German artillery, which had crossed the
Scheldt at Termonde, opened fire on the column. At
the first explosion the startled horses reared up. The
old man fell, and his foot was crushed. "Forward,
march! . . ." shouted the officers. Such episodes as
these occurred all along the ranks of the interminable
procession. It was autumn; the days were growing ever
shorter, the nightmare hours of darkness ever longer.

Many of the refugees crossed into Holland, and so
relieved to some extent the retreat of the army. The
Dutch authorities did the best they could to provide
for them. Never had there been within modern times
a retreat on such a scale in Europe. Without counting
the thirty-five thousand soldiers from Antwerp, the
number of Belgians who crossed the frontier from
Maestricht to l'Ecluse is estimated to have been one
million. For the first time since the sixteenth century
the people of Belgium threw themselves into the arms

of their old enemies in the North. In the villages of Zeeland-Flanders the Protestant churches opened their doors to the refugees, who slept there on the straw. Abraham Hans, the Flemish novelist, stood up in one of the pulpits and recited to them the glorious deeds of the Belgian army. They listened to him spellbound as they lay exhausted on their pallets, while the speaker could see, from where he stood, the set and impassive faces of the Calvinistic farmers of the district, who were seated on the benches.

The army had to pass through the meshes of the far-flung German net. One hundred and fifteen thousand Belgians reached France. Two hundred and fifty thousand crossed the Straits. The King and Queen were in the midst of this upheaval. They spent one night at St. Nicolas, another at Selzaete, and another at Eecloo. No one knows what their thoughts were during the long agony. The black-clad gendarmes of the escort and the thick red beard of their leader, Major Blampain, were a familiar sight. The King never lost his troubled expression; personal danger left him unmoved, but when the safety of those around him was threatened, his anxiety was manifest. At breakfast he drank coffee with his officers and treated them with friendly cordiality, but as time wore on he gradually grew more serious and inscrutable. This G.H.Q., where the red breeches of Major du Roy de Bliquy and Lieutenant Lancksweert struck the only note of colour amongst the sombre green and black uniforms, was the gloomiest and sternest of all the Belgian headquarters during the War. The Queen, like the King, had dis-

pensed with all her personnel, and had only retained
Countess Ghislaine de Caraman Chimay, her gallant
companion through all the vagaries of fortune.

The weather was fine. Beyond the Canal of Ghent
at Terneuzen, the dust raised by the feet of the refugees
was less thick. At last the retreating troops were able
to find marching room; and at Eecloo the King, whose
nerves had almost reached breaking-point, said to Major
du Roy: "Let us ride to Bruges, but not by the main
road; it is too crowded. We will go across country, and
the cars can meet us at the gate of the city." The
Major had an hour to plan out the route before he
galloped off; in the King's company the pace was fast
and furious.

The country round about Bruges is delightful, with
its sandy soil, woods and tiny villages. At every little
farm a dog chained to a kennel barks wildly, standing
guard over pump, midden, and the wood-heap stacked
high for the winter. The houses are all alike except
that the shutters are painted to their owners' fancy.

Bonfires were being lighted in the meadows, from
which rose the not unpleasant reek of smouldering
vegetation. Peasants stared uncomprehendingly over
the hedges at the small band of riders, preceded by two
officers in busbies, who rode straight on as if they had
known the country all their lives. At the village of
Maele, they found the Queen's car which had just arrived. Refreshed by his ride, the King and his companions dismounted. The closed cars awaited them.
In silence they drove through the sleepy old town which
had been startled from its dreams by the sound of

wheels, the rumble of the last trains, and the voices of
the Flemish soldiers raised in song as they marched by.

The King and Queen went to their villa at Ostend.
The iron vice tightened round them. Alone, in their
immense villa, haunted by memories of Leopold II,
they sorrowfully gauged the extent of their loss. Family, houses, those places where they had worked and
played—all were lost to them. The town was a chaos of
exhausted troops. One boat after another bore away
the sick and wounded; officers, men, stragglers in search
of their units, formed an inextricable imbroglio against
the background of a pleasure-fair in this brilliant late
summer—Casino, bodegas, merry-go-rounds, café chan-
tants, all the blatant and gaudy décor of an expensive
watering-place where high revel is held till dawn. A
few racing yachts were still lying at anchor. Among
them the King recognized his beloved *Ibis,* on which
he had lavished so much care.

The faubourgs of Ostend are like landscapes by
Utrillo, with cafés, barracks and indeterminate waste-
land, each field melting into the next. Zeebrugge lies
to the north, and Nieuport and La Panne to the south.

One morning the mounted gendarmes of the suite,
with their wide black cloaks, trotted at low tide across
the sands to the south. Even Ostend was endangered
now.

On October 14, at the Villa Crombez at Nieuport,
the King drew up the order for the day, and then pro-
ceeded to the trenches. He saw all the commanding

officers in turn. Here are the actual words of his Proclamation:

SOLDIERS,

For two months and more you have been fighting for the most just of causes, for your homes, for national independence.

You have held the enemy in check, undergone three sieges, made several sorties, and carried out a long and difficult retreat. Up till now you have been alone in this immense conflict. You are now fighting side by side with the gallant French and British armies. It behoves you, with that courage and endurance of which you have given so many proofs, to uphold the reputation of our army. Our national honour is at stake.

SOLDIERS,

Face the future undaunted, fight on bravely. In the position in which I have placed you, may you look straight ahead, and call him a traitor who speaks of yielding unless a formal order shall have been given.

The time has come, with the help of our powerful allies, to drive from the soil of our beloved country the enemy who has invaded it, regardless of his pledged word and the sacred rights of a free people.

ALBERT

After he had issued this proclamation the King went to Furnes. On October 15, while the rain was beating down on the red roofs of the town, he made a calculation of what troops remained to him: eighty-two thousand men and forty-eight thousand rifles. Where and how could this handful of soldiers hold out?

In this amphibious country, as the Breton writer, Le Goffic, has said, "it is not enough to beat back the

sea which would otherwise swamp it twice a day with regular tides; it is also necessary to stem the rivers that rise in the clay hills of Houtland, stagnate on the impermeable soil, flood the meadows, overflow the roads, and cut off the villages. . . . Only scientific drainage can cope with the water that oozes everywhere, making pools that glimmer in the fields all the year round. . . . The northwest winds, that harry the skeleton trees till they crouch low in fear, drive before them storm-clouds of icy rain from the hyperborean regions. And when the rain ceases, a thick white mist rises from the earth. . . ."

During those days, Dunkerke was a pitiful sight. Crowds of peasants, panic-stricken by the German advance, had evacuated western Flanders. This country, the most peaceful and anti-militaristic in the world, was doomed to be a vast barracks for four years. In the meantime the unfortunate refugees fled southwards, mingling with the columns, as had happened between Antwerp and the Canal of Ghent-Terneuzen. In the heart-breaking manner of all refugees, they had heaped up on carts all that seemed to them most precious.

But if the civilians burdened themselves, the soldiers, on the other hand, lightened their load. They flung away all their kit into ditches, only keeping their rifles and cartridges; the roads were strewn with discarded spades, as if the first impulse of the weary infantry of 1914 was to get rid of their clumsy entrenching tools which were to be the continual instrument of their safety for four years. At Dunkerke, soldiers and civilians met in indescribable confusion. Huge posters were

THE SOLDIER KING   Wide World

put up there, instructing all Belgian military strays to
report to the two local barracks. The soldiers obeyed
instinctively, with the fatalism of lost men who are desperately seeking for a roof to shelter them, an officer to
lead them.

Unfortunately, there were many young recruits who
would have made excellent officers but who had not
yet received their sergeants' stripes, while in the barracks at Dunkerke there were harassed and exhausted
old generals, awaiting orders. The reform of the high
command was proceeding of itself, and the shortsightedness of politicians was hastening the sacrifice of the unfortunate leaders. On the other hand, General Wielemans was absolutely in his right place at the head of a
group of brilliant young staff officers. A rapid purge
was going in the regiments. The Battle of the Yser was
to be won by Colonel Jacques, Colonel Meiser and
Colonel Biebuyk, young and resolute men, whom
neither responsibility nor physical weariness could
daunt.

None of the powerful Allies of the King fully realized
at this time the terrible plight of the Belgian army.
Neither M. Augagneur, First Lord of the Admiralty,
who had been charged by the French Government to
make a report, nor Colonel Bridges, the British Military Attaché, an optimist of the de Broqueville type, a
simple and straightforward man, grasped the situation.
Not even General Foch himself gauged the actual condition of the Belgian army. Right up to the fifteenth
of October they had been utterly mistaken. The sixteenth was the first day of horror.

On that day, when the Belgian army had taken up "spade and trowel," Foch was at Furnes. For the first time the great King and the great General were to meet. No one yet knew what their relations would be in the future, but everything pointed to the conclusion that they would be strained. Foch acted like a whirlwind. The unbounded imagination which inspired him was in strong contrast with the mind of the King, which was caution itself for others, utter recklessness where he himself was concerned. Part of the King's strength lay in his ability to confront events with a stony impassivity. Foch, on the contrary, could not restrain his feelings, and would thump on the table loudly enough to wake the dead. When the officers of the Belgian G.H.Q. saw him coming, an icy shiver ran down their spines. Instinctively, Foch always spoke of the offensive; and the King on the Yser felt that only one resource was left to him—to die amongst his men in the mud of the trenches.

Foch lavished advice, of which, though some was excellent, the main part was impracticable. He had said to the Belgians: "Dig yourselves in"—purely fanciful advice to those who knew the soil of Flanders, as wet as a sponge, and criss-crossed with streams from Dixmude to Nieuport. Foch would never willingly admit that he was wrong, but he would change his opinions in a flash. The King took a long time to come to a decision, but once his mind was made up, nothing would alter it. Above all, Foch was never able to understand that he was dealing with a King who was as proud of his army as a mother of her children. To

Foch, one division was as good as another; to the King, where a Belgian soldier was concerned, there was no such thing as a common denominator.

They spoke different languages. The King had a great admiration for Foch, but he would as soon have entrusted one of his battalions to the Grand Turk or the Grand Lama. To sum up, the King listened to Foch and understood him perfectly well. Foch listened to the King and only half understood him.

On October 20, Ronarch's marines repulsed an enemy reconnoitring expedition on Dixmude. An infantry attack was made on the bridge-head of Manekensvere, a short distance from Nieuport. It was obvious that the entire German offensive would be concentrated on the Belgian front. On the twenty-second the German heavy artillery was placed in position. The Allies realized the quality of their adversaries. These had been recruited amongst the immense army of volunteers who had flocked to join up at the first signal for mobilization. A million young Germans had followed on the heels of the enthusiastic and eager men to be first mobilized, and had rushed to the recruiting offices. Some of them were hardly out of their teens. All were going through that state of nationalistic fever of which the youth of Germany was again to give such extraordinary instances during the course of the years. They had been sent to camps, where they had been "broken in" in a fortnight; and at the end of September they were organized and ready to fight like the most hardened campaigners.

These were dark days for the King. The advance posts were falling one by one along the entire right bank of the Yser. The marines, like the rest, had evacuated their position. Dixmude alone still held fast, obstinately defended by the 11th and 12th Regiments of the Line and Ronarch's Brigade. From all parts of the front, the information of prisoners and deserters showed that four fresh army corps, Nos. 22, 23, 24, and 25, were joining up with the 3rd Reserve Corps, the 4th Division of Ersatz, the 44th and possibly the 43rd Divisions. The entire French army in the Ypres sector agreed with the Belgians that the next few days would see a German offensive on the grand scale.

It came with such force that from the twenty-first, after an enemy bombardment of unparalleled violence, all the Belgian reserves had to be brought into action. Thenceforth, Colonel Wielemans was obliged to tell the King that apart from the men in the trenches he possessed not a single soldier. The hurricane of shelling raged all through the night of the twenty-first to the twenty-second. On the evening of the twenty-first, when the French liaison officer went to Colonel Wielemans for orders, the latter gave him a note for General Foch and General Joffre, which ran:

"The situation in to-day's bulletin is extremely serious: all our reserves are in action. The line of the Yser may be broken either at Dixmude or near St. Georges and Schoorbacke to-night or to-morrow. It is absolutely essential that we should be supported on the right, and that reinforcements should be ready to strengthen the position wherever necessary. Our men have under-

gone an uninterrupted bombardment and severe attacks on a twenty-mile front for the last four days. We have only fifty thousand rifles at our disposal (including marines).

"The concentration of the French division to the north of the Furnes-Nieuport line is of no help to us, and the Belgian army cannot guarantee that it will be able to hold the Yser."

Alas, in the early hours of the twenty-second the German troops broke through the line of the Yser in the zone of Tervaete. The communiqué had not exaggerated the gravity of the situation. That morning the Franco-Belgian co-operation reached its crucial point. Foch, with one of his impulsive gestures, despatched the 42nd Infantry Division, under General Grossetti, to Furnes; but it had strict orders not to leave the Furnes-Nieuport sector. This was the Division that he intended for the coming offensive. It would have answered perfectly had an offensive been possible at such a moment. Under Foch, Grossetti's infantry had covered themselves with glory on the marshes of St. Gond. When they had landed at Dunkerke, Foch had had the happy idea of ordering one of the battalions to march past; and when Joffre paid a visit to the King at Furnes on the morning of the twenty-first, Grossetti's 15th Battalion marched past the two leaders with such irreproachable precision and rhythm that they were profoundly impressed. But these troops were not to stir from where they were; Joffre would not consent to send more than three battalions with artillery to the firing line. The rest of the Division was not placed at the

disposal of the King, and remained inactive. And the bridge of Schoorbacke had just fallen.

Thus, on the twenty-third, the Belgians sustained the entire attack. Most of them had already been three days in the trenches. Fifty thousand men on a twenty-mile front clung with ferocious tenacity to the last inches of their native soil. They were in an unspeakable state, exhausted and caked with mud from head to foot, and it seemed as though they would be buried there forever, in the drizzle that soaked them to the skin. For nine days on end the sky had been grey and overcast, without a single break on the horizon. There was no solitary ray of light in a nightmare that looked as if it would never come to an end.

To crown all, there was growing discord between the two commands. The French high command had put General de Roussel d'Urbal at the head of the army of the north; he was an extremely distinguished cavalry officer, but as stubbornly prejudiced as Foch himself. News came from Chantilly that the German troops at Tervaete were advancing in open order; but the French liaison officer, Colonel Brécard, realized that this proved nothing. At length, he took it on himself to go to General d'Urbal and implore him to send the 42nd Division into action. But d'Urbal refused to listen, and the Colonel could only inform the Belgian G.H.Q. of his failure, where (as he himself says) his "communication was coldly received."

At length, at ten o'clock on the twenty-third, the French Colonel sent a message to Furnes that during the night one of General Grossetti's brigades, with artil-

lery in support, would advance in the region of Tervaete.   That same night a party of seventy Germans
crept stealthily into Dixmude, which was in pitch-dark-
ness.   They were discovered and attempted to escape;
but Surgeon-Major Duguet, several sailors and Le Hel-
locq, the chaplain, were killed.   Major Jeanniot was
also killed by the German commanding officer in a
hand-to-hand fight.   Some of the German raiders, in
their fear of being captured, had butchered their prisoners.   Ronarch had them shot outright.   The battle-
field had become a jungle where men cut each other's
throats by night.

October 24, 1914.   On that day, those Belgians who
did not believe that Providence had any good in store
for them might well have thought for a moment that
all was over.   Colonel Brécard noted: "The front is on
the point of giving way on all sides . . . it looks as
though it will be impossible to avert catastrophe. . . ."
Foch arrived that night, as resolute and aggressive as
on the first day.   He still spoke of an offensive.   Grossetti, fully aware of the situation, laid it bare to him.
Foch saw the King, saw Colonel Wielemans.   He used
grandiloquent language to both of them, and held forth
in the same heroic strain to the officers.   But it seemed
as though this great soldier, who usually brought victory with him, was speaking to deaf ears.   Even General d'Urbal himself had no illusions left.

The King preserved his miraculous calm.   All who
lived through those sinister days have remained under
the spell of his simple and superb majesty.   In such
moments, he, and he alone, took command; and be-

neath the rain of shells, when the roofs of houses crashed
to the ground around his headquarters, he seemed to be
silently avenging himself on the century of political
fetters by which his dynasty had been bound. Now he
could be a King indeed. All that was not heroic had
receded from him; he seemed to have been born to this
vocation, and to have been called by long aeons of experience to give his utmost on this day when everything depended on him.

The situation was so grave during this last week of
October that the King, who now spent all the day and
part of the night at Furnes, telephoned one morning
to La Panne. There Elisabeth, attended by her lady-
in-waiting and one aide-de-camp, was awaiting word of
Albert's death under fire. The officer answered the
telephone. The King's voice said slowly:

"You must leave with my wife. Go as far away as
possible, but remain on Belgian territory . . . you
must start at once."

The officer returned to the Queen and informed her
of the King's command.

"I refuse to go," she said point-blank.

It was obviously so useless to oppose her that the
officer hesitated . . . then chose the simplest way for
a soldier, and said:

"In that case, Madame, I shall have no alternative
but to ask His Majesty to relieve me of my present
duties to the Queen, and send me back to my regiment."

He looked so wretched that the Queen smiled and
gave in. Loth as she was to leave her post at the front,

she fully realized that at such a moment she must not add to the anxiety of the King and the army. She left La Panne that evening, thoroughly determined to return as soon as possible. She stayed at Proven, near Poperinghe, in a château that had escaped the shelling, and left it eagerly as soon as the war sky brightened. Then she was no longer an added anxiety, but a solace and an inspiration. All those who saw her during that crucial week divided their admiration between her compliance with the national discipline and her rooted determination to stand by her country in its heroic effort.

At two P.M. on the twenty-sixth, Colonel Wielemans gave a general outline of the situation. The Chief of Staff was deeply moved as he informed the leaders of the allied armies that the Belgian army was at its last gasp, as was Grossetti's brigade. Colonel Brécard, who represented Foch, "listened in frozen silence to the mournful recital. . . ." The discussion dragged on and, in view of the "disastrous" information, the first orders for an evacuation were drawn up. None of these was sent. Brécard said in a low voice to Colonel Wielemans: "What does the King say? Has he been told?" The Colonel let it be understood that, before going further, he had thought it best to hold this conference, the results of which he would communicate to the King. The French colonel withdrew. It was four o'clock. At the end of every hour he sent a liaison officer for news. At seven o'clock, this officer returned and announced that all plans for retreat had been can-

celled. The King would have none of them, and had torn up the proposals submitted to him.

Just as a sick man who has received Extreme Unction sometimes returns to life, so the Belgian army which had been *in extremis* felt its pangs grow less severe. On the night of the twenty-sixth, Foch telephoned that the 9th Corps was attacking Poelcapelle, and would then proceed in the direction of Staden-Cortemarck. The Germans put up a strong resistance, but these attacks relieved the Belgian front. Here things continued to calm down in a horror of blood and mud. Dixmude was a nightmare rendezvous where the wounded— French marines, Belgian soldiers and Senegalese troops —were huddled together pell-mell in unspeakable filth from which a loathsome stench arose. It was an inferno of bursting shells; even the pouring rain could not quench the fires that broke out. Dixmude . . . so great is its glory that we stand breathless before the heroic impulse of a people who offered themselves to their King, and the greatness of that King who gave himself to them.

In the opposite trenches, the Germans were weakening—they, too, had almost reached the limit of their endurance.

At length, on the twenty-seventh, the scheme for flooding the country was put into practice. Writers have said that during these ominous days Foch had been the first to utter the word: "Inundation. . . ." He had indeed pronounced it, but in connection with the sluices of Dunkerke. Had this been carried out, the Belgian

army would have had the surging water behind it, and
would have been cut off in that direction. The Belgian G.H.Q. and Baron de Broqueville had thrown up
their hands in horror at the suggestion.

But the flooding of the Nieuport sector was quite
another matter. With the skilled assistance of a lock-
keeper, Major Nuyten discovered the key to the labyrinthine sluices which command the Beverdijk. All
that had to be done was to open them at a suitable
moment, and then close them at low tide. The operation was not carried through without difficulty, however. The King ordered the Belgian army to fall back
to the railway embankment. The open sluices in this
embankment had to be sealed tight. There were at
least forty-two of these. The tide came slowly through
the so-called Furnes sluice, and on the twenty-eighth it
rushed through that known as the Zuidvaart. Within
two days the water had reached the entire German
front. The trenches were flooded.

Slowly the sea did its work, washing away the ammu-
nition, driving out the men, engulfing the observation
posts and even the outposts, whose defenders were compelled to surrender. At night a thick mist rose from
this desolate ocean, as if the very elements were saying
to the Germans: "You shall not pass. . . ."

It was only just in time. On the twenty-ninth, Grossetti's division underwent in its turn the horrors that
Colonel Wielemans and his troops had endured. Worn
out by days of suffering, Grossetti was profoundly depressed, and was outwardly all the more calm because

despair was gradually overwhelming him. The men had made a superhuman effort. Admiral Ronarch was talking to one of his officers on the road to Dixmude when he suddenly saw him close his eyes, sway, and fall at his feet in sheer exhaustion. The Admiral remarks that he was not in the least surprised. All his officers and he himself were at the end of their tether. Ramscapelle was taken. But that same evening it was retaken. This was on the thirtieth. The battle was nearing its end.

On November 1, President Poincaré, General Joffre, Lord Kitchener, Millerand, Ribot, Jules Cambon and M. de Broqueville were dining together at Dunkerke. Joffre was firm in his belief that the War would only last six months. Kitchener retorted that it would go on for at least a year. M. Ribot spoke of financial considerations. It was beyond them all to foresee the course of events. Only heroism counted. Prophecy had become futile. The next morning, at Adinkerke, the King received the President. At last he was certain of being able to welcome visitors in his own realm, on the soil that his ancestors had bequeathed to him. Everything was quieting down in the front line; the fighting was shifting towards Ypres. The President, who was deeply moved, found words to tell the King of his unbounded admiration for the work that had been accomplished. Two cavalry regiments, one Belgian, the other French, were stationed at Furnes. Foch arrived on the following day. He was already speaking of a great offensive in the East.

Throughout those ten days the regiments of the Yser were as wild in appearance, as scantily fed and sheltered as the vast, chaotic hordes of the Retreat from Russia. Like them, they were ragged and verminous. They ate what they could find—cattle which had strayed from burning farms and which had fallen victims to the shrapnel. Soon even this come-by-chance food was lacking—the hen houses they passed were empty. On the twenty-fifth, Admiral Ronarch was forced to drink brackish ditchwater. Some of the soldiers chewed their emergency rations to get their teeth into something. "The men are reduced to the state of animals," wrote Admiral Ronarch. "I myself have nothing to eat—I left my provisions behind with my horse. I live on what people give me out of kindness, and they have little enough to give." During the night of the twenty-sixth the mail-carrier brought letters for some of the French soldiers, but they were unable to read them because lights were strictly forbidden. The Belgians received no letters. And it rained, it rained hopelessly, as if this downpour would go on forever. On November 18, when General d'Urbal reviewed the marines, he did not recognize their Admiral in the midst of the scare-crow apparitions whose feet protruded from their boots and who carried blankets of startling hues, picked up God knows where. They were like spectres that bore no likeness to anything human—all that remained to them was the will to live.

Every man may draw his own conclusions about this battle, which ranks as one of the most heroic in the annals of the War. But to quote a French officer, Gen-

eral Azan, who kept the historical records of that army:

"Beneath his retiring and unassuming exterior, Albert I was the soul of the War against the invader. He restored confidence to his soldiers when they were weakening, he opposed the decisions of his high command when they did not uphold resistance to the death. Sustained by the strength of a wife in every way worthy of him, he has been a great King to his country, a King to whom history will do homage.

"To the Allies, he was the calm, thoughtful, chivalrous colleague who, without any ostentation or fuss, carried out a strategic manœuvre on which possibly the fate of the War depended. He closed the gate of the north to the German invasion and kept it closed, with troops who had reached the breaking-point, until help came."

An officer was despatched to Nieuport. It was now certain that there would be no more concentration on the line of the Lys. The King, in full command of the situation and free from all political worries, had seen his Ministers depart without regret. They had left by mail-boat for Le Havre; conscious of their futility, these worthies vaguely realized the absurdity of their situation. M. de Broqueville alone could still be of use, and he had established his headquarters at Dunkerke. The King hesitated between Furnes and La Panne. He spent a night at Nieuport Bains with M. Crombez and his daughter, the Countess de Romrée de Vicheret. "What will become of us? What shall we do?" asked his devoted hosts in anguish, and the King had to smile

and put a world of optimism into his voice as he answered: "All will be well—your King is with you."

He himself was deeply depressed. All those who saw him during those desperate days were struck by his resolute but hopeless aspect. He would have liked to stay at Furnes, but it was explained to him that General Headquarters had already been established and that his going there might cause inconvenience. He realized that this was sound sense and went to La Panne. An officer preceded him and asked a worthy in the village square where he could find the burgomaster. He had addressed the burgomaster himself; and that notable pointed out three large villas that were to let. One of them, the property of M. Calmayn, was still tenanted by the entire domestic staff. The Queen had retained two of her ladies-in-waiting; but the King, with that pioneer spirit which often moved him, had dispensed with all his retinue and had arrived without a single servant. The officers took possession of the two neighbouring villas; and so the new life began.

CHAPTER VIII

IN OCCUPIED BELGIUM

THERE was an Intelligence Department in Brussels under Baron Capelle, one of the heads of the Foreign Office. Through his agency all essential information was transmitted to La Panne. It is impossible to say how many messengers managed to get through the barbed-wire entanglements which cut off the north of Belgium. They hid at night on the moors of the Campine or in the furrowed fields of Flanders, waiting for a signal; when all seemed clear, they took their lives in their hands and hacked their way through the wire.

Documents continued to accumulate on the King's writing desk. Contrary to the belief prevalent among his ministers at Le Havre, the King knew to the full all the sufferings, the agony and death that made up the toll of horror in occupied Belgium. . . .

Four years. The life of captivity endured for four years under the yoke of von der Goltz. The Governor was old and obese, his face was spotted and scarred, and "he looked at you slyly through shining round lenses, which gave him an almost jovial expression." A diplomat in uniform was in charge of foreign affairs. This was Baron von der Lancken. The Field-Marshal had suddenly decided at Namur to appoint him to his staff. "His sleek black hair, small moustache, easy manners and *soigné* appearance showed him to be a man of the

world . . . he was suave, correct and punctilious, but always on his guard; he kept a wary eye on the world about him, conscious that an ambitious man must everlastingly be on the *qui vive*. . . ." But when all was said and done, both he and von der Goltz were wretched and helpless victims of bureaucracy at war. They were not highly esteemed by their own countrymen. Germany treated them with indifference, the civilized world with execration.

From the very first days of the occupation, it was obvious that the economic straits in which Germany would shortly find herself would be a crushing blow to Belgium. German soldiers were heard to say that if they themselves died in the trenches the Belgian civilians would very soon die of hunger. The Germans were not concerned with the needs of any but themselves. The various municipal councils, however, had already organized communal kitchens; and Ernest Solvay, the founder of the Economic Institute, had set up a Central Committee that dealt with cases of distress and hunger in Brussels.

But no effort would avail unless large quantities of wheat arrived from abroad. There would soon be no bread, for the wheat grown in the country was sufficient to feed only a fifth of the population. Would Germany sanction the importation of foodstuffs for Belgians, once she had found it difficult to provision her own troops? Fortunately, common sense made it plain to her that occupied Belgium must have food-supplies;

that a starving Belgian population would only create further trouble.

The Ministers of the Neutral Powers who had remained in Brussels agreed to act as honorary presidents of the Committee. This was the sole means of keeping the Germans in check, whilst at the same time inspiring confidence in foreign exporters. There was no civil authority in Belgium. All power would be vested in the man who was able to take the reins. For the first time since 1830, a national mediator was to be appointed. There could be no question of a general election, still less of any recommendation from the Government at Le Havre. The hour of agony awaited a master.

That master was Emile Franqui. Since those far-off days when he had taught at the Military School, Captain Franqui had travelled all over the world. At Hankow he had laid down railroads, negotiated with Mandarin governments and bandits, and had floated enterprises in which iron and coal were employed to the profit of Belgium. From the United States, he had brought back a very accurate conception of American idealism and American materialism, as well as of the constantly shifting enthusiasms of the American people. He had negotiated loans with J. Pierpont Morgan on behalf of Leopold II, and, on his return to Belgium, had himself become a banker—a director of the Société Générale of Belgium, the most powerful financial house of the country. Here, when he had passed his fiftieth year, he took it easy after the stress of colonial life.

Though he knew very little about books, he knew

volumes about men. He used to say he had made a
thorough study of the five types of mankind: white,
black, red, yellow—and the men of Antwerp. But above
all, his adventurous character had brought him into
conflict with other great enterprisers of his type—sometimes to his cost. It was this element in his past that
made it possible for him to send Mr. M. K. Shaler, an
American engineer living in Belgium, to London in
October, 1914, to meet a brilliant mining-engineer, also
an American, with whom Franqui formerly had had
dealings in China. This mining expert was Herbert
Clark Hoover. Captain Franqui had known him fifteen
years earlier. It was said that their association had
ended in a quarrel, and that these two bulldogs had
parted with bared teeth.

Hoover had come to London in the spring of 1914 to
draft a scheme for the Panama-Pacific Exposition, and
had remained as president of the committee which dealt
with the repatriation of Americans who had been
driven out of Europe by the War. On October 17,
M. Franqui, accompanied by Baron Lambert de Rothschild, went to see him at his hotel. The two recognized
each other instantly; but now their private differences
were forgotten.

Two days later a first cargo, consisting of two thousand, three hundred tons of flour, rice and beans bought
in London, reached Brussels.

In November, 1914, Hoover went to Brussels for the
first time. Brand Whitlock received him at his office
in the Rue de Trèves, in the heart of the Quartier Leopold, the Belgravia of Brussels, where, alas, the cars

that had streamed past in the sunny years were now but few under the leaden sky. In this provincial city, whose monotonous streets are a series of large, discreet houses, the great Commissioner arrived with his colleagues. Buried deep in an arm-chair, Hoover spoke in resonant tones. By the luck which falls only to the share of very large enterprises, a body of financiers who were willing to give their services for nothing had associated themselves with him. "He had a sensitive face with the drawn expression of a man who is expending too much nervous energy," wrote Whitlock; "deep-set black eyes that sometimes had a fixed stare, and a high white forehead over which his hair fell carelessly. . . ."

For two hours, Hoover fired questions at Whitlock. The following day the Americans and the neutral ministers were received by the Committee in the offices of the Société Générale in the Rue Royale. All the notable Belgians in the country were grouped round Captain Franqui. Old M. Solvay presided, and addressed a speech of welcome to the Americans. When he reached the words: "We are a small nation . . ." his voice broke, he could not continue, and there were tears in the eyes of all those present. It was the first time that tears had fallen at a board-meeting of the Société Générale.

A few days later the habitués of the soup-kitchen in the Rue Blaes received a strange visit. The Rue Blaes, the most picturesque slum in Brussels, is in the heart of the Marolles—a kind of workman's Montparnasse, crowded with cafés, culs-de-sac, tortuous alleys and dance-halls. It is the haunt of dog-breeders and pigeon-

fanciers. The women who sell mussels, piping-hot snails and "chips" speak an appalling Franco-Flemish dialect known as Marollian. A rough and hearty crew swarms în these lower depths, like a republic of *enfants terribles*. None but the Little Sisters of the Poor are immune from the jokes, personal remarks and pranks of the light-fingered young hoodlums, who are called *ketjes*. The German police only ventured there on tip-toe, fully aware that when the roughs slouched out of the *bistros* where they had been drinking *Lambic* [1] watered down with syrup, the patrols were liable to be bashed over the head, or kicked in the stomach—the classic procedure of Marollian pugilists. An exceptional treatment was meted out to this haunt of bookies and chisellers, *zinguewes* and accordion-players—in fact the Germans dared not smash the gramophones which emitted loud metallic "Brabançonnes" at night under the darkened lanterns, while the mussel-sellers shouted shrilly the length of the gutters. There one morning in the Rue Blaes, beside a convent, the poor were standing in a queue when they saw Herbert Clark Hoover, Whitlock, Franqui, and Rockefeller's representatives approach.

The soup-kitchen was in one of the many dance-halls; it contained a mechanical piano and was decorated in the gaudy style of a carrousel. It was a picture of hunger parading in the soiled satin shoes of cheap and tawdry pleasure. Shivering under the livid sky the crowd entered the hall, and filed past the steam-

[1] A strong Belgian ale, known as Moeder Lambic (Mother Beer).

ing saucepans with the resigned look of those who are at least certain that they will not starve. Slowly they moved on, under the pitiful gaze of all the great captains of adventure who had given themselves wholeheartedly to a task that would never yield them a franc or a dollar.

Within two years the Relief Committee had at its disposal a fleet of two thousand, three hundred and thirteen cargo boats. By amazing good luck, only seventeen of these were torpedoed and only fourteen were mined. According to Professor George J. Gay, the total import figures reached five million, one hundred and seventyfour thousand, four hundred and thirty-one metric tons. Between them, Hoover and Franqui had cut through the jealousies of friend and enemy alike.

In conjunction with M. Franqui, M. Solvay, and the rest of the Relief Commission, the diplomats played their beneficent part. Thus Whitlock entered into the history of Belgium, in company with Villalobar. The latter, in the course of an argument on the subject of a convoy of provisions with a Geheimrath who had scant respect for him, exclaimed: "I am not a corn-chandler!" A corn-chandler, indeed! The essence of the man was in those words. There had never been a Castilian Marquis who was more of a Marquis and more of a Castilian than he.

Rodriguez, Marquis de Villalobar y Guimarey, had passed a sad and lonely childhood in an invalid-chair— his limbs were grotesquely deformed—and would have sunk into a state of melancholia had not his aunt and

god-mother, the Empress Eugénie, lavished special care
on him. But, as though to compensate for his physical
disability, he possessed extraordinary strength of character, and a brain whose susceptibility was heightened
by his pathological condition. He had been appointed
Spanish Ambassador in Brussels on the eve of the War,
and it was known that he had been in Washington in
an advisory capacity.

His choice was a great stroke of good fortune for the
Belgians. At the onset of hostilities the Germans had
believed that Villalobar was their declared friend; and
they were only half-mistaken. This allowed him to in-
tercede for numbers of poor creatures whose lives would
otherwise have been lost. In the interests of the Relief
Committee, he often undertook highly dangerous journeys across the submarine-infested waters. M. Franqui
was amazed by his courage and soon made firm friends
with the Marquis; for energy and a sense of duty were
enough to cement the intimacy between these two men
who had come from such opposite poles.

His American colleague had come forward spontaneously for quite another reason. Brand Whitlock, who
had formerly been Mayor of Toledo, Ohio, on a Reform ticket, was a scholar, writer and lawyer. He was
unusually tall and lean, with a thin-lipped, sensitive
mouth, and was invariably to be found in the company
of his quiet, unassuming wife and his "two mothers"
(his wife's mother and his own)—"Gentle old ladies
who had lived through the Civil War." He adored
children—the more so, perhaps, because the cradle in
his own home had always stood empty. By tempera-

ment Whitlock was as little suited to the conditions of war and the task of mass provisioning as he was the rôle of a gangster. Yet it was he who became the guiding spirit of the Relief Committee, to which he had introduced Villalobar when the latter had decided to see the War at close quarters. Whitlock was as tender-hearted as he was generous, a democrat in the real sense of the word. During those terrible years, he even found time to talk of literature and to add to it.

When Whitlock's mission in Belgium finally came to an end in 1917, with the entry of the United States into the War, he went to La Panne and saw the King and Queen for the first time since 1914. The King asked him if he would like to visit the trenches. This was perhaps the most amazing episode in Whitlock's career: he was one of the only diplomats of the belligerent countries to have visited officially both sides of the front —the German line with von Bissing, and the Belgian dug-outs with Albert I.

Whitlock was to live many more years, a little bewildered, it may be, by his own lot. The tired heart of the old Ohio reformer had rekindled to life in the warm affection of Rome. He loved Cardinal Mercier like a father; and after he had received the Primate in his house, he wrote: "Cares, ugly thoughts, obsessing fears, vanish before the Cardinal, and we feel ourselves in the presence of the eternal verities. It is as though a prophet has crossed our threshold, and our hearts seem to burn with a more ardent flame."

During Whitlock's lifetime the Brussels boulevard that was a continuation of the Boulevard St. Michel

was called after him. One day a six-year-old child said innocently to its mother: "Why must we always walk along the Boulevard St. Michel? Why can't we go down the Boulevard St. Whitlock?" It was an apt canonization.

The German Governor-General, the old warrior von der Lancken, was not a bad sort. He was more artless than brutal. He had been charged by his Emperor with the governing of Belgium, and believed his instructions implied that he must also bring her morally to her knees. The ludicrous side of this undertaking entirely escaped him.

Hence the paradox of the German Occupation of Belgium. These gentlemen had penetrated into a country by the sole right of might; yet no sooner had they settled down than they set themselves seriously to the task of converting their victims to the beauty of the German cause. All the vicissitudes of the administration during those four years are explained by this extraordinary pretension. But for this, neither the long correspondence with Cardinal Mercier nor the involved proceedings before military tribunals would be comprehensible.

Interminable palavers went on between Lancken and the Civil Administration. At times, M. Franqui lost patience and let fly. On one occasion, utterly beside himself, he shouted: "You are treating us like slaves!" Lancken, who was completely worn out, exclaimed: "I cannot allow you to say things like that."

Fats were scarce, and the trams creaked and groaned

along the streets. Grass grew up between the paving-stones of the Quartier Leopold. Belgium's Chief Rabbi preached a sermon in the Synagogue, in which the Amalekites bore a singular resemblance to the Germans. As they feared him less than they did the Cardinal, they promptly clapped him into prison.

The slave-hunters continued to make raids. Droves of Belgian workmen were despatched to Germany like so much cargo, and Lancken knew exactly what Captain Franqui had meant by saying: "You are treating us like slaves." Theodor, the distinguished barrister, was imprisoned. The notables who were still at large sometimes foregathered. Dinner parties were occasionally given, but the men did not dress. On July 21 a crowd of patriots filed past the statue in the Place des Martyrs, set up in memory of the dead of 1830. One by one, they approached and flung roses, carnations and garlands of ivy tied with crape into the shallow stone trench that surrounded the monument; for several days it was filled with a mass of blossoms. Thirty-four thousand young men crossed the frontier after heroic journeys, climbing over or hacking their way through high barriers of barbed wire charged with a deadly current: thirty-four thousand Odysseys across the plain of the Campine. Those anguished waits amidst the bracken, those resorts to the wiles of poachers—all this makes up a saga of student heroes that has not yet been told.

And there were heroes, too, from among the professors. In particular, one recalls the gallant history of M. Henri Pirenne, a Walloon from Verviers—the most celebrated professor of the University of Ghent. He

had studied at Berlin and Leipzig; he held honorary doctorates from several foreign universities; his great work on the Middle Ages in Belgium had been published originally by a German house. In his learned retreat, with his square shoulders and leonine head, he was not unlike an intellectual Franqui.

M. Pirenne had passed his fiftieth year. His three eldest sons had enlisted. One, a corporal in the Grenadiers, had been killed at the battle of the Yser. The professor only went out for exercise, or to meet a few of his colleagues at the Café Bass in the Marché aux Oiseaux. There he voiced his opinion of the invaders with the surprising volubility which characterized him.

During the first days of the Occupation, a young professor in field-grey had come to ask him for a short interview on the causes of the War. Trimborn, a deputy of the Reich, had tried to persuade him to give a series of public lectures. A similar attempt had been made by several German professors; and Dr. Hoeninger of Berlin had expressed to M. Pirenne his sorrow and surprise to find him acting as a *bitterer Feind*—a bitter enemy of Germany. The first experiences of this kind had caused the professor to fly into uncontrollable rages, but he had finally grown accustomed to them. M. Pirenne continued, however, to make incautious utterances.

On March 18, 1916, an officer arrested him at his house. The next morning he was sent to the military camp at Crefeld.

In an officers' camp at Crefeld, in another at Holzminden, in the midst of Flemish, Russian and French

workers and students, M. Pirenne did battle in his own way. In the filthy huts, crawling with lice, the great scholar from Ghent once more gave his lectures on the history of Belgium to a breathless audience, who sprawled on flea-ridden mattresses in the dust gilded by pale German sunlight. Anyone who followed his classes in Ghent can easily imagine how fervently, how movingly, he spoke. Never had he had more absorbed listeners. President Wilson and the President of Princeton wrote personally to the Kaiser to ask for M. Pirenne's release. But the professor continued to fight.

In this strange university, M. Lebrun, a workman from Liége, had set up a printing-press under the floor boards of hut 73. On July 21, 1916, it turned out hundreds of photographs of the Belgian King; and the tiny portrait was cherished as a talisman by the crowd of men, women and children from France, Russia, Poland and Belgium. On that Independence Day it was impossible for all of them to be present in the tiny wooden chapel, for this would have aroused suspicion; nevertheless, Belgians of every type and class gathered together, their national historian in their midst. "None of those who were there," he writes, "will ever forget the expression on their comrades' faces when the words *Domine, salvum fac regem nostrum Albertum* rose up within the bare wooden walls. . . ."

Did the King, isolated in his headquarters at La Panne, dream of the touching prayer the prisoners gathered together in the camp at Holzminden were offering up for him?

The spectacle of the honourable Baron von der Lancken arguing with the Cardinal, and opposing the philosophy of Kant to that of St. Thomas, is astounding. The inherent absurdity of these discussions must have afforded the great prelate many glorious moments of intellectual jubilation.

When an ordinary criminal has committed a crime, he pleads either "Guilty" or "Not guilty." The German Government, however, tried to follow a third course. It meant to convert its victim and, in every case, to argue with him. How far did it intend to pursue this policy? No one quite knows. Most extraordinary of all is the fact that it actually crossed swords with the Cardinal Primate himself.

In a country as deeply religious as Belgium, the Archbishop is a power that cannot be discounted in any sphere. There are many matters, no doubt, in which he will declare he has no say, but these are mere words, and the very voicing of them is proof to the contrary. There are only six dioceses in this country of nearly eight million souls; but they are souls that pray, in which unbelief is rare; and even free thought is permeated, in spite of itself, with faith.

Of these six dioceses, the arch-diocese of Malines is the most powerful in the Catholic West, from the point of view of its works, schools and congregations. The University of Louvain is dependent on it, and its immediate influence is exercised over a people one-half Flemish, one-half Walloon—over Antwerp and Brussels. You will find that Belgium revolves on the spiritual axis of Antwerp-Malines-Brussels. By a happy chance,

the Catholics of Belgium had allowed the principal
Bishopric to remain at Louvain, long before there had
been any talk of a linguistic frontier.

In 1914, the Bishop of this ancient Burgundian capital was a Walloon of Brabant. He came from the people, was very tall, extremely handsome, an aristocrat by
nature. Everything about him was symbolic. Born in
a poor and crowded Belgian parish, he was plebeian by
origin, Roman through the friendship of Leo XIII,
European through his cultural relations, but over and
above all a priest. Like the humblest curé of the humblest hamlet, he never wore anything but the soutane.
Those who touched it, touched all the soutanes in Belgium—and their name was legion.

Cardinal Mercier was a professor. He had formerly
been Head of the great seminary, the organizer, on the
advice of Leo XIII, of the Higher Institute in Louvain.
He was well acquainted with the world of international
writers; even better with that of the priests and professors of his flock. He had already published a large body
of work in serious reviews, written both in French and
Latin, and directed mostly against the materialistic
creeds and myths taught in German Universities.
Thus, this disciple of St. Thomas might become a dangerous polemicist, the more dangerous because he
would lure his adversary into unknown territory—the
territory of doctrine. He seemed to have derived all
that characterized him from St. Thomas, his spiritual
guide: a commanding presence, fluent speech, compel-
ling eyes, and a gift for repartee which made him as
much a militant as a mystic apostle. He had seen Wil-

helm II once, when the Hohenzollern had visited Brussels in 1910. The Kaiser had been icy with him, either because he sensed a hostile power, or because he disliked the Cardinal for his merciless attacks on German scholars.

The first meeting between the Primate and von Bissing, the Military Governor, went off more or less smoothly. The Cardinal, who had been called to Rome in August, 1914, for the Conclave of Benoît XV, had returned to Belgium by way of France and England. Von der Lancken received instructions not to antagonize the Cardinal, but to keep a discreet and assiduous watch over him.

As the Palace of Malines was in ruins, Cardinal Mercier installed himself at Antwerp and did not return to his devastated home until December. From there he wrote a letter to Cardinal Hartmann, the Archbishop of Cologne, which he confided to von Bissing with the request that he would see that it reached its destination. The letter was an admirable and vehement philippic against the German allegations of sharp-shooting, and particularly against a speech made by Bethmann-Hollweg. The Chancellor's outburst was denounced as a "tissue of lies." Naturally, the letter was never sent. But then, on December 25, when Christmas Day was being celebrated in every church in Belgium, when the Germans were making merry round the fir trees they had stolen from Belgian forests, the priests were informed that they would receive a pastoral note entitled *Patriotism and Endurance*.

The pastoral note contained a terrible indictment, in

which the entire German responsibility was established point by point. The great deeds of the Belgian army were described, and the duty of the population toward the invader was defined thus: "This power is not a legitimate authority; therefore, deep down within yourselves, you owe it neither consideration, fidelity, nor obedience." On the thirty-first, von Bissing was made acquainted with the text of the note, and despatched von der Lancken to Malines.

In his memoirs the diplomat admits that this was the most painful episode in his career. He left by car in the middle of the night with two officers of von Bissing's "Personal staff." He was empowered to *use his authority* with the Cardinal, should it be necessary. When he reached Malines, Lancken had no difficulty in discovering the printer of the pastoral note, "who, moreover, made no attempt to deny anything and was arrested." As for his visit to the Cardinal, Lancken chose that moment when least attention would be attracted—just before early Mass. It was still dark when he was admitted into a vast, icy apartment on the ground floor. Lancken the diplomat had grown accustomed during his stay in Rome to what he called "impressive ecclesiastical apparitions"; but he had never seen the Cardinal. Almost immediately, the Primate entered, unconsciously producing a sensational effect. "It was quite unpremeditated," writes Lancken, "the inevitable result of the situation, with no striving after theatricality."

Lancken plunged straight into the matter in hand. He was far too intelligent to underestimate for one mo-

KING ALBERT, GENERAL PETAIN, AND PRESIDENT POINCARÉ IN THE MEUSE DISTRICT

ment the adversary with whom he had to deal. His main object was to get the Cardinal to agree to an interview with von Bissing, in which case he would not be compelled to *use his authority;* and should there be any scandal, he would be relieved of a thoroughly distasteful task. He achieved his purpose with considerable adroitness and, greatly reassured, left the huge glacial chamber where he had been scanned from head to foot by one who looked like a prophet of old.

The Governor trod delicately, "in order not to make martyrs or rupture relations with the Curia." The priests read the pastoral letter on January 1, and were left unmolested. It was a tremendous capitulation, both for von Bissing and his master. Instead of issuing orders, they were condemning themselves to discussion and, considering the nature of their opponent, that might lead them into deep waters.

And there, indeed, was exactly where it did lead them. *Patriotism and Endurance* was followed by the *Call to Prayer,* wherein the Primate wrote, on the solemn anniversary of the Battle of the Marne: "Let all devout souls continue to pray; let them protect our troops in their prayers with the shield of St. Michael, the Victor inspired by Right." St. Michael is the patron saint of Brussels; his golden effigy stands on the Hôtel de Ville. Poor Lancken now attempted to play the part of good angel. He went to Malines, where he offered to restore the Cathedral of St. Rombaut. The Cardinal gave him a point-blank refusal; and there ensued involved discussions on the psychology of the German people.

1917! In a Parisian drawing-room, during that year of dwindling morale, Baron Beyens heard the significant remark: "The silence of God passes all understanding." But at that moment there issued from Malines a Lenten Mandate: *"Courage, my brethren,"* inveighing against all partisans of peace at any price. Von Bissing died on April 18, 1917, in the château of Trois Fontaines. The Cardinal wrote to Lancken that he would pray for his soul.

But the Cardinal's great stroke had been delivered on July 21, 1916. The German authorities had forbidden the *Te Deum* to be sung in St. Gudule. A solemn service was held in its stead. After the Gospel had been read, Cardinal Mercier appeared with his mitre and crozier. His passage to the pulpit was like a scene from the Apocalypse, so many were the radiant or anguished faces turned to him in ecstasy. In simple words, he proclaimed that the hour of deliverance was at hand, and ended with a *Per Crucem ad Lucem.* It might have taken place in one of the early Christian Catacombs. When he had finished speaking, the organ began to play the "Brabançonne," softly at first, then swelling into a triumphant crescendo. The congregation broke into tumultuous shouts of "Long live the King!" The German police battered at the doors of the Cathedral, but the churches had once more become inviolate sanctuaries; and the suave diplomats who surrounded old von Bissing were fully aware that they had been cast for the insufferable rôle of barbarians.

CHAPTER IX

LA PANNE

THE King's residence at La Panne stood in the midst of a sandy waste where the salt wind never ceased to blow. Before it lay the sea, behind it a battlefield.

The Queen, who was nearly always in white or blue, was restless, indefatigable, forever busy. The King, immensely tall, dressed in black when he first arrived but afterwards in khaki, would walk about with his hands behind his back, silent for the most part. When he did speak, he spoke very slowly.

At low tide, soldiers drilled on the sands between the sea and the dunes. The King would be on horseback, the Queen too; she generally wore a light grey habit. Sometimes they would be joined by Prince Leopold. The troops formed fours under a sky that seemed to melt into the ocean; and the murmur of the waves made fitting music for this epic scene.

We can picture it for ourselves. The wind blows away the orders shouted by a Colonel: "Officers, N.C.O.'s . . ."; the bugles ring out, and the notes rise into the air and seem to disappear like larks on the wing. The tiny Queen sits upright as a statue on her huge horse. When she returns to her improvised Palace with the King and her household, she sets the pace, invariably a gallop, up over the dunes, down into the

pannes (hollows).   Unconsciously, her daring shows her love for the theatrical.   When they reach the villa, she dismounts, gathers up her habit, and goes in, her husband at her side.

As soon as they had received permission from their parents, the Princes returned from England.   They were slim, high-spirited boys, up to all manner of pranks among the sand dunes.   There was a pond with a raft and poles, where they used to paddle about to their hearts' content.   Sometimes, Prince Charles would overbalance and get an unexpected ducking.   Princess Marie-José would play about amongst the coal heaps and earn a scolding for having spoilt her pretty shoes.

The days were growing very short, and the acetylene lamps had to be lit early in the afternoon.   Wild duck flew across the sky, heading southwards, and winged their way towards the front, where the officers, crouching in shell-holes, would bring them down with their rifles.   The English monitors ceaselessly came and went. The King had resumed his life of study.   Newspapers and reviews were once again heaped on his table.   His life was divided between General Headquarters at Furnes, his visits to the trenches, and La Panne.

He never went on leave.   I look through the Royal calendar from 1914 to 1918.   Never once did the King take a holiday on the Côte d'Azur, never once did he go to Paris or England for recreation.   Riding was his only diversion.   Every morning, when he was not in the trenches, he rode, either with the Queen or with an officer, and this draught of fresh air in all weathers was as indispensable to him as sleep and work.   When

silence brooded over the countryside, it was too much akin to his own melancholy. Meadow succeeded meadow as far as the eye could see, intersected by gaping ditches full of reeds that sighed and swayed. When the breakers crashed, the murmur of the rushes made a mournful undercurrent of sound. The King would be sunk in his own thoughts for hours at a time, until his insatiable thirst for knowledge woke him to life again. Then he would ask his companion of the moment question after question, displaying great interest in his personal affairs. He was always inclined to look on the black side of things, always ready to turn the point of any argument against himself. The rides were taken simply for the sake of exercise. The King understood human psychology, but he had no conception of the nature of horses, treated them like cars, and set them much too fast a pace. He could not play tennis or golf on account of his near-sightedness; so he galloped for galloping's sake, regardless of his own weariness or that of others.

As some distraction was necessary, the whole household had taken up or resumed the habit of riding. At first the hundreds of rabbit-holes had proved dangerous pitfalls, but the Moroccan contingent had soon organized beats. Moreover, the Belgian guns were dragged by dogs, those large, docile beasts that are still to be seen every morning harnessed to milk-carts in small towns. These dogs soon helped themselves to any rabbits that had been overlooked by the beaters, and gradually the burrows disappeared.

A cross-country chase was organized. Even M. In-

genbleek took part in it, for it was literally impossible
to live at La Panne unless one rode. The secretary was
a crazy rider, quite oblivious of danger, and would return to the stables at the same break-neck pace at which
he had set forth. "We will lend you whatever you like,
M. Ingenbleek," the officers used to say. "You can even
borrow our toothbrushes—but not our horses!" He
had been warned that when he came to an obstacle, he
must pull hard on the rein, close his eyes and dig his
knees into his mount. He obeyed to the letter, jumped
enormous ditches, landed badly, and came down in the
mud, bespattering saddle and bridle. As these were
the property of General Jungbluth, stormy scenes frequently ensued.

The Queen, who was a fine horsewoman, and whose
mount responded to her slightest touch, delighted in
these riding parties. They formed the great topic of
conversation at the officers' mess and led to general
hilarity. Major Galet alone did not join in the laughter. Yet he rode every day, as solemnly as if he were
saying his prayers in a church as silent and shuttered
as himself. The King, who was given to bursts of gaiety, who could laugh heartily at a joke, and who in certain moods enjoyed a little spicy gossip,—the King preferred the company of this gloomy adviser to all the
rest. Galet, the dull and honest soldier, the wet-
blanket, reputed to be the bearer of all ill news, was
unanimously believed to be the subject nearest to his
master's heart.

Days succeeded days, weeks followed weeks. With
morbid desperation the King would reiterate: "You see

—I told you so. . . ." He had been right when sub-
consciously he had been aware that the War would not
be over in a day. Even when he was at Antwerp, the
King had felt that the War would be of long duration.
One of his aides-de-camp there, a cavalry officer, had
spoken to him of his regret at not being able to fight
in the front line. With disconcerting slowness, the
King had replied: "The War will not be over in a day.
. . . You will command a regiment."

He believed in the virtues of his people and his army,
saw red when anyone ventured to disparage them, however slightly, and would not allow any criticism of them.
Nor would he allow any criticism of the King—save by
the King himself. But he fully made up for the voices
he had silenced. Morbidity has been described as the
ego turned against itself. The King possessed this
temperament to an exaggerated degree. Whence had
come this deep-seated preference for all that was sorrowful? Optimists invariably rubbed him the wrong
way. Pessimists, too, would arouse his anger, and he
would stigmatize them as "birds of ill-omen." Yet their
plaints penetrated his black moods and echoed endlessly
in his brain.

All was antithesis in the character of this giant among
men. He knew that he would go down to history for
the great deeds he had done—yet he everlastingly de-
rided himself. He found it hard to believe in inspiring
news—yet he was the glorious inspiration of heroes. All
that he touched became noble and serene—yet he invariably reiterated: "I have read so-and-so's article—he
thinks I am a fool." When discussions arose, he was

cautious,—cautious to excess,—yet when the Battle of
the Yser was at its height, when the Allies could not
agree and panic was everywhere, he alone had turned
the tide of victory.   His spirit of disbelief was only
equalled by his courage, his spirit of criticism by his
incredible coolness in the face of death.   In peace-time
he instinctively put off difficult decisions until the following day; yet during war-time he never hesitated,
went straight to the point, and saved his country.   In
such moments he forgot his intellectual doubts, the
fruits of too much study.   He was wholly and solely a
hero; and his serene and eager acceptance of this superhuman condition is irrefutable proof of his innate
heroism.

During the first winter there were many visits, all
of them official.   The Prince of Wales was the most
frequent guest, and Albert developed a liking for his
young cousin's conversation.   He studied him with
lively interest.   "He is charming—not intellectual, but
very intelligent and full of common sense," he told his
friends.   Of all the Saxe-Coburgs, the Prince of Wales
was the one he liked best, and he felt a personal satisfaction in claiming him as one of his own family.

The King of England and President Poincaré paid
official visits.   After this, the Spartan severity of a mar-
tial régime once more prevailed.   Those were hard
days.   In the holidays the Duke of Brabant returned
in his Eton suit.   Both he and his brother were spring-
ing up.   With that curious instinct which causes sons
to imitate their father, they already walked with their
hands behind their backs and slouched along with a

slight stoop. They lost this habit later on, but I have photographs taken at La Panne in which the three figures, one big and two small, are standing in exactly the same way.

The needs of the army were now being supplied on entirely fresh lines. Shiploads of equipment for the troops began to arrive along the coast in December. At Antwerp the King had been in communication with a personage of a Leopoldian cast of mind, who proved to be a most fortunate acquisition. Owing to his important position in the business world, Baron Empain was the very man to become a great army contractor. The director of a number of electricity companies, and of the Metro in Paris, the owner of an entire township in Egypt, he had connections with all the right people. In a short time, sandbags, guns, lorries and trench material were acquired through his agency at a very reasonable figure.

In exchange for his valuable services the great millionaire asked for a very small reward—he wanted military rank. He was gazetted first Colonel, then General, then Lieutenant-General and aide-de-camp to the King. At last the patriotic financier was able to don the uniform he had so often worn in his dreams. At La Panne, he proved to be a most valuable addition to the officers' mess. He had brought with him the best chef in Paris, who managed a welcome change in the monotony of the daily menu.

The Belgian army owed to Baron Empain the great munition works at Le Havre, where, by the end of the

War, twenty thousand workers were being employed. The Baron came across many of his old associates in uniform. He secured the appointment of Colonel Theunis of the Artillery (who had retired from the army and gone into business) as head of the organization for purchasing goods from London. With unexpected good luck, Colonel Theunis was steadily climbing every rung in the ladder which began at the promotion class in the Military School and ended at the Premiership. After the War, many officers were to leave the army for a business career, and pass from M. de Broqueville's sphere into that of Baron Empain.

Every Belgian banker in London rendered whatever service lay in his power. Amongst them was the enigmatic figure of Alfred Loewenstein. After he had carried through an extremely useful deal, he succeeded in obtaining a commission in the cavalry, and was thenceforth known as Captain Loewenstein. Much as he desired it, however, he was never invited to La Panne.

Lord Curzon came on a visit. Though everything pointed the opposite way, the King had become greatly attached to the Marquis. He knew him to be a snob, was aware that he was arrogant and ostentatious—the very antithesis of himself, in fact. But it was noticeable that the King always preferred men with whom he had nothing in common. Kindness itself, he cared for many whose natures lacked this gentler side. Full of consideration for his servants and the humblest of his subjects, he was tolerant towards the few men of his acquaintance who dealt harshly with their inferiors. Cur-

zon's chief characteristic was his conceit, and the King had none. Though holding very large views, Curzon had a passion for detail, and ran his household on the most economical lines. The King never thought about money, and never once in his life gave a thought to the drawing up of a menu or to any other domestic matter. Yet he was extremely fond of Curzon; he admired his brilliant vice-regal ability, and enjoyed hearing him talk about his residence in India, and about the vast interests of the British Empire. Curzon went to and fro, and basked in his own importance. The King, for his part, had too Olympian a consciousness of his own dignity even to dream of any rivalry. He feared the bourgeoisie, laughed at the world of society but was perfectly at his ease with statesmen, and above all with autocrats. I shall have more to say about this unexpected facet of his character.

Lady Asquith's visit was a different affair altogether. The wife of the British Prime Minister turned up one afternoon uninvited, and the officers were obliged to offer her a room in their villa at General Headquarters. They were not a strait-laced set, but it took the new guest only ten minutes to throw them into complete confusion. She walked briskly into the hall and announced that she wanted to lie down. Clad in an extraordinary waterproof that looked like a panther skin, she went upstairs complaining that she was dead tired after her crossing. When she reached the top, she called to Major du Roy de Bliquy:

"Do you speak English?"

"Very badly, Madame."

"That's no answer. When do you dine?"

"At any hour that suits you, Madame."

"That's no answer. At what time?"

"At eight o'clock, if that will suit you, Madame."

"Good."

At eight o'clock, she came down in a very décolleté frock, to the stupefaction of her mess-mates who were all in uniform. Since August 4, 1914, they had not once dined in Belgium with a woman in evening dress.

Next day, she went to visit the King and Queen, who had also invited the Earl and Countess of Athlone. Lady Asquith flung her arms round the Countess's neck. No one knows what took place in the royal drawing-room, but the King always chuckled when he spoke of it. Margot came back in a state of great excitement, and burst out to the officers:

"I've seen your King. What a marvellous head he has! I was dying to kiss him, but I hadn't the nerve, so I kissed the Countess of Athlone instead!"

Her visit lasted three days. Before she left, Margot presented all the officers with pull-overs, knitted in England. These were of such good quality that they refused to wear out, and are still in use! Her departure was a fitting climax to her stay. In the presence of the King, the Queen, and the British officials, she enthusiastically embraced Captain Lanksweert who was showing her to her car. The Queen was highly amused, and thenceforward persisted in calling the Captain the Kissed Officer. It was the brightest interlude La Panne experienced in four years.

There were evenings when the King and his household could look to seaward through their windows and see epic battles in progress. One night, they heard a confused uproar coming from the calm sea—the sound of engines going at terrific speed. All they could see were lights that came and went. Two British destroyers had met six German destroyers. Taken by surprise, the young British commanders ordered full speed ahead and rammed the enemy. The British destroyers managed to sink two German craft apiece; the other two made off.

Every form of warfare was to be found in this region—war on earth, by sea and in the air. The King loved to go out on a destroyer; he would seat himself on the poop where, in rough weather, the waves rose so high that they washed completely over him. Both he and the Queen had a passion for these expeditions, out of which arose their great friendship with Admiral Keyes, the hero of Zeebrugge. Unknown to their personnel, they cruised with him in search of submarines. Dr. Nolf only learnt of these adventures because the King returned from one of them with a severe attack of bronchitis. These risks he ran at sea were danger signs of the risks he was to run in the future on the mountains; yet it is easy to understand how a man like the King exulted in such exploits, in the call of the open.

There was never anything in the nature of a party; there were no entertainments or recreations. Riding and walking were the only antidotes to the weary hours

of work. The King would go for long walks in the country, in the company of some devoted friend. The officers of the household still amuse themselves by reckoning up the time they spent in striding across the soil of Flanders side by side with the King. Whether he spoke, or whether he was silent, his thoughts wandered far afield. Often, far too often, as he took the road from La Panne to Calais, he would say between his teeth:

"This is where my grandfather landed in Belgium. This is where they would like to drive me out."

It would never strike him that such mournful remarks might cast a gloom over his listeners, and he would stride on, perpetually chewing the cud of his bitterness. Nine times out of ten he would increase his pace almost as though he were running a race. His heavy boots would ring out loudly on the soil of his country, and after a few minutes the officer beside him would be sweating at every pore. "I'm not tiring you, am I?" the King would say, kindly, and his companion would rather have died than admit that he was out of breath. In this manner they would return to the villa, where the sentry presented arms. The King would slow down and return his salute. He would then go to his study, strengthened and rejuvenated, where he would slit envelopes open and bury himself in abstruse books.

He had gradually given up smoking his execrable Italian cigars. He drank nothing but water after 1915; and as he grew older, his dislike of gluttony was extended to those who indulged in it. Although he never

condemned any form of human weakness, he could not
endure the old gentlemen who delighted in food and
helped themselves twice to each dish at a banquet.

Under his sway the villa Calmayn became a kind of
monastery. The Queen might fill it with souvenirs and
knickknacks, might quicken it with her inexhaustible
vitality—life there remained austere. At times, func-
tionaries announced the presence of society people well
known in Brussels and Paris, and enquired if they
should be given audience. The King simply shook
his head and said: "Mere waste of time." The country
was at war. The servants had acquired the tone of the
house. Henriette, the groom, Belfroi, the head stable-
man, Van Dyck, the valet, and the impassive M. Pierre,
the major-domo, went to and fro, like lay-brothers in a
monastery. The officers might laugh at mess, but in
the King's antechamber they remained motionless for
hours on end, seated in accordance with Jungbluth's
maxim: "Sit when you can. . . ." A few society
nurses and fashionable women gave dinner-parties or
musical soirées. Some of the aides-de-camp innocently
accepted their invitations, but soon realized that these
affairs were disapproved of in high places. The country was at war. Galet, that anchorite, remained un-
tempted in this Thebaid. The King sometimes laughed
at what he thought was a pose; hypocrisy was what he
abominated above all else. But though he himself
might laugh at Galet, he would allow no one else to
do so. The country was at war. Davreux went on
dangerous expeditions with his photographic outfit, and
returned at night with his spoils. One morning, he

ventured out with a new camera, climbed to the top of
a parapet, clicked the shutter—and was instantly shot
through the head. The war dragged on. On Sundays,
early morning Mass was said in the parish church and
on some afternoons the Jesuit Father Hénusse would
give a discourse. There were nights when La Panne
was so heavily bombarded that the King, concerned for
the safety of the Queen, insisted that they should leave.
They went to Les Moëres, an hour's journey away. On
the very first day, shells fell all round their house.
They shrugged their shoulders as they listened to the
explosions.

The Queen was the sun of that grey winter. It was
she who relieved the officers of their tasks and took
them with her on shopping expeditions to Dunkerke.
She went incognito, full of mischief, taking pleasure in
mystifying people. "Look at that enormous French officer," she would say to her aide-de-camp, "he's a freak!
He's even taller than my husband. Go and ask him
his height." Her aide-de-camp would bring back the
information, and they would dash giggling into a shop.
On two or three nights she had stolen out with the
Countess of Caraman. These were dramatic escapades,
for the régime was strict for women on the Belgian
front, and they had to produce their papers at every
moment. Elisabeth laughed at every misadventure;
those who surrounded her knew all her little ways, and
of her predilection for dangerous visits to the trenches.
She had absolutely no time-sense, and had an engaging
habit of forgetting what o'clock it was. Her unpunc-
tuality was notorious; so, too, was the King's familiar

gesture of taking her by the arm and leading her back, much overdue, to the villa, murmuring as they went along: "Come, Elisabeth, we're late—we must hurry." But he would walk quite slowly, for she was the only person in the world who could stop him from taking those famous strides of his; he would suit his step to the tiny paces which were all she could manage.

In the evenings, when it was low tide, they would stroll across the sands and gaze towards the north. To-day, the Belgian soldiers, remembering these things, often say: "We should never have won the War without them."

The Queen grew more and more addicted to her visits to the trenches. When the King was with her all went smoothly, but when she went with Major du Roy de Bliquy all sorts of daring schemes came into her head—risks which the distracted officers had to think out a thousand ludicrous reasons to dissuade her from taking. The trenches were approached by endless zig-zag passages, and at every bend unknown faces would appear, wreathed in smiles. Often a fresh outburst of shells would screech in the air above the head of the visitor. A dug-out had to be instantly indicated to her, where she would fling herself, laughing.

In the evenings, she would sketch in the little salon, amusing herself by drawing the portrait of some officer or other. This was a constantly repeated scene. Major du Roy would be seated in a corner, the Countess of Caraman beside the Queen at her working; and the King, with his hands behind his back, would pace to and fro, only stopping to bend over the sketch and

say: "You've made his nose too short, Elisabeth . . ." or "Elisabeth, he's much balder than you've made him. . . ." Smoking was permitted, but he himself had long since given up coffee, liqueurs and cigars. He would stride tirelessly up and down like a monk in the cloisters.

It was at this time, in the midst of heavy bombardments, when the sirens at Dunkerke nightly heralded the approaching saturnalia with "chromatic wails," that Pierre Loti saw the Queen. It was a bright Sunday morning. The Queen had also invited a hundred waifs and strays (who were being cared for near by, and in whom she took a great interest), and a number of nuns—those heavy Flemish nuns whose parchment-like faces are creased by lines of laughter. The little boys, who were dressed as miniature soldiers, and the small girls, were drinking chocolate and eating bread-and-butter in the Queen's villa; they sang songs and danced. The King, at the conclusion of his interview with Loti, led him into the midst of this pastoral scene and introduced him to the Queen, who was wearing "a simple frock of embroidered blue silk, and a tiny blue toque fastened to her hair with a sapphire-headed pin."

Loti was shown over the Queen's bungalow, the queerest Trianon imaginable; "one of those movable contrivances made of pine-wood which can be shifted from one place to another in an hour or two, like a nomad's tent." The Queen had grown wallflowers between the stunted bushes. The bungalow was "entirely hung with delicate blue Persian silk, relieved by a touch of rose colour, scrolled with a large design representing

the porticoes of a mosque. It contained nothing in the way of furniture but a writing-desk and divans, on which were piled bright-hued cushions."

The conversation was entirely confined to Benares and the Hindu religions. By tacit agreement no mention was made of the enemy. The Queen's lady-in-waiting was dressed in yellow silk. Cats wandered in from the village to prey on the nightingales. The gendarme, who had been detailed to keep them off, ran past clapping his hands and making as much noise as possible. This "cat incident" amused the Queen, who explained the reason for the commotion to Loti, the great lover of cats. Next she took him for a walk in her wood, her poor little wood of stunted fir trees, pointed out her nightingales, and picked him one of the flowers that "grow on the sand-dunes and blossom on the Isle of Oleron, a kind of large mallow with satiny yellow petals and a subtle scent." Night was falling when Loti left her, "the night that threatened her with so many dangers, despite the ecstatic trilling with which her tiny feathered protégés would presently swell their throats amidst the heavy thunder of the guns."

The most privileged of all the visitors received by the King during those years was President Poincaré—privileged not because he was the recipient of many confidences, but because of the outspokenness of his statements. Like the King, the President was unassuming and cautious. He too was bound by the iron fetters of a constitution at which he fretted incessantly, but,

like the King, he guarded it as if it had been a precious talisman.

The two leaders confided to each other their beliefs, hopes and anxieties, as they climbed the tower of the Hôtel de Ville at Furnes, or sat in the salon at La Panne, where "a huge fire blazed up the wide chimney." They visited Houthem, where General Headquarters had been established in a farmhouse, and Loo, whose ancient story the King narrated with an antiquarian's knowledge (". . . it is the only Flemish town that has the Roman Eagle on its coat-of-arms"). At Chantilly, where he paid a return visit, the King remarked ironically: "What makes the task of a leader of a state somewhat involved is, that when things go smoothly the Ministers are congratulated, and that when they go wrong the King and the President are the scapegoats." In March, 1916, at La Panne, he said: "When I act, I am accused of exceeding my rôle and of poaching on the Government's preserves. When I do nothing, my inaction becomes a source of reproach."

I am not at all sure whether the King was pleased when Poincaré subsequently published these disillusioned confidences of his, but he certainly gave utterance to them; and Poincaré neither omitted nor added a single word, not even when he noted that on May 21, 1916: "The King is always gloomy and preoccupied. He can no longer foresee the issue of the War. Moreover, he dreads, as he has repeatedly told me, revolutions in the future." No, Poincaré certainly did not invent these words, nor did he imagine this sentence: "The sea here

is beautiful, but there is too much wind, and the flowers
are few and far between."

Nothing, however, had prepared these two men to
exchange confidences. They had met for the first time
in 1912, during the course of an official visit. The
President had quite erroneously imagined that the King
had a "Flemish accent." He had been charmed by the
Royal children. In 1915, he asked nine-year-old Princess Marie-José, in the presence of her parents, whether
she remembered Madame Poincaré and himself. "No!"
—she replied, with disconcerting frankness, to the great
embarrassment of her mother and father. At that time
the Princes were in England, and their mother rang
them up every day on a line specially reserved for her.
This was guarded by French territorials, and the President received her gracious thanks for this service.
Thus, friendly relations were carefully maintained.

In a fit of depression the King remarked to Poincaré:
"I remember a time when the Socialists were making
progress everywhere, when all the leaders of the State
were threatened, and I thought that none of them
would remain in office until the end of the War. Now
things are better, but we are all placed in a false position. I am asked to act in person, and I have neither
the right nor the power. I constantly receive unpleasant letters from people who are amazed that I am not
directing affairs, that I do not call my Ministers together. . . ."

In July, 1917, the darkest hour, ugly rumours were
afoot. It was said that the King and Queen had betrayed their country. Whence came these reports?

What secret treachery had insinuated them even into
military circles? They had actually reached the ears
of General Anthoine in his Headquarters at Haze-
brouck. Who told the King and Queen? They seem
always to have been the first to learn of the most puerile
accusations. General Anthoine thought it his duty to
inform the President, who went immediately to La
Panne, on that sunny July 21. The King understood
at once the motive for his visit. He spoke indignantly.
"It has been said that the Queen has been to Switzerland where she met some of our enemies. I wish to
inform you, M. le President, that she has not visited
Switzerland since the outbreak of the War. She has not
set foot in that country." "I believe you, Sire, and this
is the first time I have heard this absurd statement
made."

Always that anonymous and suspicious *They*. "*They*
say that . . ." "*They* accuse me of . . ." Even old
pre-War gossip was dished up and endlessly masticated.
"Why does M. Cambon imagine that before the War
my Government and I were in favour of an alliance
with Germany? He has said a number of things to Baron
de Gaiffier on these subjects which have greatly surprised me and deeply wounded me. My wife and I
have always loved France. I begged Beyens in November, 1913, to warn you of what was going on in the
Kaiser's mind. I myself warned you when I went to
Paris. Need I say more than that from that time forth
all my sympathies were with France?"

On February 2, 1918, when the King went to visit
the Italian front, the French President noted: "The

younger of the two Belgian princes has had an acute
heart attack. The Queen has been ill for a long time.
The King himself badly needs rest. . . . He is anxious
as to what repercussions the Russian Revolution may
have in other countries, Belgium in particular. He is
uneasy about the German machinations amongst the
Flemish, and complains that the British forces are making too many attacks on Antwerp and other occupied
Belgian towns. . . . He does not believe that the War
will end this year."

The War was almost over, yet at La Panne its end
seemed more distant in February, 1918, than in February, 1915. News came of a vast upheaval in Russia,
and of the assassination of Nicholas II. The Czar had
formerly been a subject for pity, but now his fate
aroused storms of indignation. "Nothing could be held
against him," said the King. "Nothing could even be
laid to the doors of Sturmer and Protopopov. Nothing, therefore, has been gained by the change." Thus
the months dragged along, and the conversations between the calm and deferential President and the philo-
sophic and anxious monarch continued. Albert reserved to himself the right to say that the War would
be of long duration, and that Germany was far from
being beaten. As has been said, both optimists and
pessimists infuriated him; the latter filled him with a
sick depression. He once heard some English officers
boasting of being able to hold out indefinitely. "They
are planting trees in Boulogne so that one day they may
rest under their shade," commented the King sardonically. He muttered sarcasms when anyone angered

him, saw red if anyone criticized him. He never realized his own greatness.

Years later, in 1933, six months before his death, he went off on his motor-cycle. He was alone, happy, as always, in his own company. At that time he was greatly interested in Austria. He assumed the name of the faithful Van Dyck, and rode from Lucerne to the Tyrol and Styria. One evening, he entered a village inn, mingled with the peasants and supped with them on bread and a basin of soup. Politics were being discussed, and "M. Van Dyck" innocently enquired what they thought of the Hapsburgs. The answers were evasive. The Hapsburgs? The Monarchy? It was all so long ago, so far off and dim. No one thought about them any more.

Night was falling. On the terrace, "M. Van Dyck" continued to talk. There was music in the inn, as there is in every tavern in Austria, and the young folk went inside to dance. Only the old people remained with the King. They began to sing. Their first song closed with an invocation to the Emperor. Their second and third airs ended with a similar refrain, a solemn and fervent hymn to Franz Josef, softly taken up by the echoes of the sleeping village. The King enjoyed telling this story in 1934, and would conclude by saying: "It's strange. These people must still think of their Kings."

If he had been able to listen in 1918 to the voices of seven million Belgians in their own country and abroad, if his sorrowful heart could have caught the sound of the united voice of his suffering and militant people,

he would have heard it ascend like an ardent and tender canticle—a song of praise far more devout than any that "M. Van Dyck" would ever hear in the remote Tyrol. But in those last weary days at La Panne so much tragedy had darkened his life that he only spoke of happiness in the past tense; and when joys to come were foretold, he scarcely listened.

In a moving poem, Verhaeren had written:

Sire, you shall return to your capital.

And the King had been grateful to Verhaeren, whom he loved, and had seen as often as he could. After their long walks in the dunes, Verhaeren had been wont to murmur in his deep voice: "How amazing he is . . . what an extraordinary character! . . ." in the simple and affectionate manner of great poets when they think aloud about the heroes of their epics. But the King no longer saw his beloved poet. Verhaeren was dead—run over by a train at Rouen, in the night, as if some shadowy demon had torn out his throat.

CHAPTER X

THE ARMISTICE

THE autumn of 1918 brought victory on all the Allied fronts, and Belgium experienced the joy of wresting back her own land from the invader. Because of its situation on the extreme west of the line of battle, the Belgian front was of supreme importance. The men proved themselves worthy of the part they had to play, and took Mount Kemmel and Houthulst Wood, which had been the objectives for many months of the Allied attacks. In 1918, the Belgian army was splendidly trained and equipped, well fitted to reconquer at the point of the sword the territory it had so dearly defended. Belgium's army had resumed its place in the great drama, but now it was on an equal footing with the armies of her Allies, and no longer wore the tragic mask of "do or die" it had worn in 1914.

In the midst of his men the King felt himself a King indeed. He held courteous but strained communication with his Ministers at Le Havre, but he was aware of a widening rift between them and the country. He himself had never been to Le Havre, for he felt that any personal contact with this parliamentary republic would lower him in his own eyes. At infrequent intervals he summoned his Ministers to La Panne. On one such occasion, when he met them at the farmhouse of Moëres to discuss the institution of universal suffrage,

his anger surged up because he felt how great a gap separated them from himself. Like Lyautey in Morocco, and Leopold II in the Congo, he had become a kind of autocrat—the result of his isolation.

The Constitution apparently vests immense power in the King. So many of its Articles begin: "The King shall appoint. . . . The King shall decide. . . . The King shall have authority to . . ." If we read no further, we should imagine that the King of the Belgians was omnipotent. But another Article nullifies the preceding Articles by saying that the King's signature shall have no validity unless it be countersigned by his Ministers. In this way Parliament reasserts its prerogatives. But during the War years, when Parliamentarianism had been relegated to Le Havre, the King seemed to be governing alone, in the midst of his soldiers. This impression was given weight by the fact that, while his Ministers were absent from the country, he himself was in Belgium, and in uniform.

In October, 1918, when the first waves of attack broke over the German trenches, the Belgian Monarchy appeared in the guise of a military and civil hierarchy—an aspect it had never worn before 1914, and which it would discard when the wheel of the War had come full circle.

The leaves had begun to turn yellow when the King and Queen went to the château of Lophem. It was a vast edifice in the Gothic style of 1880. At a first glance it struck them as bizarre, but later they found it somehow touching with its towers, glazed windows, ecclesi-

astical décor, and its weather-cocks which squeaked all
night long.

Towards 1880, when the Religious War was at its
height and passions had been unloosed, a certain Baron
van Caloen had erected this hugh red-brick building,
with out-houses in keeping, in the midst of the woods.
The château boasted a lake and an impressive gateway.
The whole effect was both ecclesiastical and feudal.
The van Caloen family had given several sons to the
Church. The walls of the huge salons were covered
with pictures of religious subjects. The series of drawing-rooms was rounded off by a conservatory. The
chapel was in the centre. The great interior staircase
would have befitted a procession of Cistercian monks.

It was pitch dark when the King and Queen reached
the château of Lophem. Gendarmes stood on guard at
the postern gate, which could be closed at night. Baron
van Caloen, his wife and eight of his children were
standing in the vast hall, which was lit by oil lamps.
The scene was reminiscent of a picture by Memling.
The King and Queen had a word for all, and listened
to the speech addressed to them by their host. He was
a man of intelligence and wit, whose handsome Spanish
profile bore a startling likeness to the faces in El Greco's
Burial of Count d'Orgaz. The Royal family were to
share the château with the van Caloens. The King
and Queen walked quickly up the great staircase, every
one of whose treads creaked. Their rooms opened on
to the garden, the tennis court and the lake.

Every morning the bells of the village church adjoin-
ing the manor summoned the faithful to prayer. This

church had also been built in the pseudo-Gothic style.
General Degoutte had established his Headquarters in
a small white château close at hand. A Benedictine
abbey, in the Italian style but also of red brick, completed the picture. There were continual comings and
goings from château to monastery, from monastery to
château, through the pine woods that had been badly
damaged by the Germans. The whole of this wooded
valley, dotted with lakes and brick-built châteaux, has
a sandy soil, and bears a strong similarity to Poland.
With the exception of the parks of oaks and chestnuts,
only resinous trees are grown there. The rye had been
harvested; it was the turnip season. Crows streamed
across the sky, forming a black edge to the dull clouds
that overhung the crests of the forests. Here, there was
no sound of the sea, as there had been at La Panne, but
the coast was only sixteen miles away, and the north
wind blew at Lophem with the same icy violence as
across the sand hills. A few yellow leaves were already
falling on the placid face of the lake, where swans sailed
majestically to and fro. The scene was typical of the
Bruges countryside. So peaceful was the château that
Pax might have been written over its gateway—that word
of greeting and blessing which is inscribed over the entrance to the cloisters in an abbey. At night, however,
the silence was broken by the loud creaking of the stairs,
which sent the officers into fits of laughter.

On the day after their arrival the King and Queen
made the Joyous Entry into Bruges. Surely that was
the strangest of all the celebrations of the Return. The
Queen in riding-habit, the Duke of Brabant in the uni-

form of a second-lieutenant, mounted their horses at the Gate of La Bouverie. This gate commands the south of Bruges—and here the King had dismounted in 1914, during the retreat.

The leaves of the chestnut trees on the walls were turning rust-red. Bruges is full of belfries and carillons, and on this glorious autumn day the bells pealed out with all their might. The narrow, zig-zag streets were thronged: men and women embraced one another, rejoicing. They rivetted their eyes on the King, the Queen and the Prince, as if they were seeing the heroes of a romance they had read a hundred times, but whom they had never hoped to behold in the flesh. All this took place in a mediaeval setting of churches, campaniles, belfries, gables and emblazoned façades.

Then came the review beneath the great belfry, amidst frantic cheering, on the site of the famous communal battles of the thirteenth century, between the house where Maximilian, Emperor of Germany, had been imprisoned, and that where the first democratic charters of Belgium had been signed. The drums beat rhythmically, making lordly reply to the far-off mutter of the guns, those indefatigable guns, that, only a few miles away, continued to sound their song of death.

Dusk had fallen when the ceremonies came to an end. The walls of Bruges are four miles from Lophem. The King decided to send back the cars and ride to the château. On their homeward journey the Queen, uplifted by the events of the day, flourished her whip. A few minutes later, belated sightseers on the road to Lophem witnessed a wild charge. "Throwing conven-

tion to the wind, despite the presence of a few foreign attachés and aides-de-camp," runs the entry in an officer's diary, "the Belgian Court rode a steeplechase. The Queen laughed unrestrainedly, and the King thoroughly enjoyed the break-neck pace." In a twinkling the cavalcade had reached the gates of Lophem. It was like the finish of the great Handicap at Auteuil. The steaming horses added their whinnies to the general hilarity. Thus ended the first Joyous Entry of Victory.

Life at the château began. The régime at Lophem was much like the life at La Panne. The King went for long walks with M. van Caloen, and they talked about trees. He walked a great deal, cycled through the woods, frequently went riding, chatted with the peasants, attended Sunday Mass, seldom laughed, spent his evenings at home, and interested himself in agriculture. In short, had he been capable of reconstructing himself, he would probably have taken his new neighbours of the Bruges countryside as a model. Yet it never occurred to him to try and change himself—he instinctively resembled them. He never dreamed of visiting anyone, and only cared for the peace and solitude of the country. One morning a bomb dropped by an enemy 'plane damaged one of the oaks at Lophem. M. van Caloen found the King standing in front of the tree. "I think we might be able to save it by cementing it," he said; and the lord of the manor replied: "Yes, perhaps if we cemented it . . ." The conversation had taken the right turn, and the bond between owner and tenant was tightened.

The King sought for subjects which would put the daughters of the house at their ease. One morning, he met one of them on the stairs, and asked: "Are you a good linguist, Mademoiselle?" She was dumbfounded, stammered incoherently, and turned to her sister, who could only say "Er . . ."

When Prince Charles returned the château became noisier. He unhooked a hunting-horn that hung on the wall on the landing, and blew it lustily. The King jumped up, burst out of his study and dashed up the stairs four steps at a time, shouting: "Be quiet, can't you! It's impossible to work with that noise going on. Oh, that boy will turn my hair grey!" The Princess took it into her head to keep rabbits, and the daughters of the house made her a present of some. Through the ventilator the little girls could see what was going on in the hall. One day, Japanese envoys came to confer the Ribbon of the Order of the Chrysanthemum on the King. The Japanese were very tiny; they bowed extremely low, hissing flowery compliments, and the King received them with a serious and thoughtful air. The children began to laugh. Suddenly they caught sight of two other gigglers round the bend of the banisters: they were the Queen and the Countess of Caraman, who smiled and nodded to them, as they slyly peeped to see if the ceremony had come to an end.

The weather was growing colder. The Queen went down with a bad attack of influenza, but she soon recovered. On Sunday mornings the whole household attended Mass in the chapel of the château. The Abbé from the Benedictine monastery of St. André, who acted

as chaplain, officiated with that simple and gracious dignity which Benedictines confer on their services. The King and Queen had their own praying-stools. M. van Caloen had asked some young cousins of his, the d'Ydewalle children, to be acolytes. When Mass was over the congregation grouped itself in the hall, and the King talked about the events of the day. It was like a miniature and friendly Versailles. When tidings were received of the state of affairs in Central Europe and the fall of the dynasties of Vienna, Munich and Budapest, the King did not hide his anxiety. "They are going too far," he said; "there is bound to be a crash. Europe is in the throes of an infectious revolutionary disease, which may communicate itself to us."

During the illness of the Queen, he said to one of the van Caloen sons: "You coughed during Mass—I heard you. You must take care; these attacks of influenza are dangerous." His conversations never lasted long. He would hasten back to the large salon, hung about with oil paintings representing scenes of Flemish hagiology, which served him as a study. And then his restlessness would seize him once more. He would jump on his motor-cycle and dash off, his engine making a frightful uproar. "It worries me—he is so near-sighted," the Queen would murmur. During these outings of his, when shells still were bursting all round, his friends would look at one another and raise their brows. But he invariably returned in a glowing mood, and no one dared to pass any comment. Only Van Dyck, his valet, would say gravely: "One day there will be an accident. . . ."

In the avalanche of events which shook Europe during those six weeks of the War, Albert retained his Spartan austerity and innate simplicity. One morning he was discovered in a field, gnawing a turnip with his strong white teeth. The Queen, who had found her bed uncomfortable, had had her small camp bed from La Panne put up in its place. They dined at night on boiled eggs, and the cook remarked: "Mon Dieu, how poor they must be! One boiled egg apiece! Mon Dieu. . . ." This barrack life had become second nature to them.

Lord Curzon of Kedleston came on a visit, and as the King was certain that the magnificent Viscount would be horrified by such monastic fare, he ordered elaborate menus. As he was equally certain that he would dislike an isolated suite, the King moved to the second floor and gave his own rooms on the first floor to Lord Curzon. Still more thoughtful was the reception given to M. Poincaré, who was the first to come and congratulate the King on having regained his country. The President was driven through the still bloodstained meadows of Flanders, and was taken to Zeebrugge, where the hulk of the *Vindictive* recalled one of the most glorious pages in the history of the British navy. The personnel of both staffs were invited to dinner, with the exception of Colonel Tilkens, who was surprised at not having been included. A rapid enquiry disclosed the fact that one of the officers from Degoutte's Headquarters had usurped his place. General Jungbluth was informed, but the French guests insisted that this breach of manners should be kept from the King.

Causes of offence were already taking shape between the officers of the different countries, and the leaders understood how wise the King had been in having obstinately refused, all through those four years, to entrust a solitary Belgian regiment to the Allied Generals, however distinguished.

One evening the Countess of Caraman whispered to her hosts: "The War will be over to-morrow. The Armistice will be signed at eleven o'clock." The thunder of the guns died down during the night. The owls on the roof hooted a response to the creaking of the weathercocks. The gendarmes, in their black peaked caps and voluminous black capes, murmured as they closed the postern gate: "To-morrow . . ."

On the morrow, two deputies drove up in a car. The Countess of Caraman told the children that the new arrivals were M. Anseele of Ghent and M. Janson of Brussels, who had come through the lines with the Spanish Consul. Politics had passed under the high gateway of Lophem in the wake of glory. . . .

In their comedy, *The Return,* Robert de Flers and Francis de Croisset have depicted a soldier who has come back from the front. He has thrown off the accoutrement of war, and his only desire is to be left in peace. But his wife, in her joy, insists upon giving parties and showing him off to her friends; she forces him into a round of gaiety, and worries him about money. No sooner has he settled down again in his home than he is obliged to discuss troublesome matters,

and wear himself out with merry-making. Could this be peace? . . . The King, in his Thebaid of Lophem, wondered a little.

When the King's thoughts went back to pre-War times, he remembered the basic laws which were in existence at the inception of Belgian politics. There were approximately one million workers in the country: those figures predestined Belgium to democracy. The strike of 1913, which had been ended by a formal promise of Constitutional reform, had been a kind of sign-post, the last landmark on the high road to universal suffrage. If the democratic hypothesis were admitted, it would be necessary to establish the legitimacy of the Flemish claims. Finally, it was more than ever requisite to bear in mind that Belgium was a Catholic country, and that a single spark would suffice to rekindle the regrettable Religious War. The Royal programme could be summed up in this formula: Counteraction and secularism.

What would be the opinion of the Belgians who had remained in the country; and above all, who would first voice it to the King? On November 10, 1918, the château of Lophem was like Noah's Ark during the last days of the Flood. Beneath a sky which gave promise of being fair the national ship sought for a peaceful haven where its royal navigator might drop anchor. No one knew who would bring the olive-branch from Brussels. Would it be better to send forth a messenger with the glad tidings, or would it be better to wait and only restore a political régime after the banners of victory had been borne back in triumph?

That the second alternative should be adopted was the general opinion in the country and in the towns. There could be no question of reinstating the Ministry of Le Havre. The very names of the Ministers had been forgotten, and their activities had been the target for sarcastic criticism and contemptuous comment. Only one name still evoked glorious memories. It was that of M. de Broqueville, the man of the moment in 1914. The news of his resignation had been received in Brussels "with consternation." He was at present lying ill with Spanish influenza in a château in Poitou. M. Gérard Cooreman, his successor, was an astute and wary citizen of Ghent, who, sensing the dangers of his position, had only accepted it on the condition that he might send in his resignation on the day that Belgium was liberated. The refugee politicians themselves admitted the perilous nature of their task. In this unsettled state of affairs, everything depended on the King.

If ever a man attacked a problem with an entirely open mind, it was Albert. To his intimates, he confessed how tired he was, what a poor opinion he had of his Ministers of Le Havre. The politicians who remained in the country excited his curiosity and anxiety. If any formula were to emerge, it would come from one of two opposite poles: Malines, where everything was drenched in mysticism, or the Relief Committee, where everything was practical and extremely progressive.

Naturally, nothing emanated from Malines, where life was on so high a plane that any activity outside the sphere of moral and patriotic duty was looked upon as

a fall from grace. Once Belgium had been liberated, the Primate would only enter the world in order to greet his victorious King with all the pomp and ritual of his cathedral. Political truth would not issue from the stained-glass windows of St. Rombaut, nor from the tapestries of St. Gudule.

There remained the Belgian Relief Committee. At its head, M. Franqui towered above his associates; his energy was dynamic; but he was a novice in political matters, and although he declared he would never meddle in them, his whole nature urged him to have a finger in the pie. His political claims were all the more debatable because they were lofty. He had lived for four years in the midst of statesmen, and had imposed his will on them to such a degree, that, had he suddenly left them in the lurch, one and all would have rushed after him and clamoured for his support. Accustomed to command, he listened attentively to the advice of experts and then acted on his own initiative, giving still more weight to expert opinion from the moment when he had adopted it as his own—it became thenceforth inviolate.

He had never been elected President of the Relief Committee by his colleagues but, since no one raised any protest, M. Franqui took it for granted that his word was law. Such was the character of the former instructor of the King, the lieutenant of the Military School, whom his pupils had nicknamed Bamboula. Of his famous promotion class, ten of the forty-six cadets had been killed in the Congo or in Belgium. The ablest survivors had become Colonels, or Lieutenant-Colonels;

and Galet, the pick of the lot, was considered to be the greatest tactician in the Army. Lieutenant Franqui alone had discarded his uniform. Indirectly he was to be spokesman to the King on behalf of the country.

What was being said in Brussels? Despite the laconic tone of the German communiqués and the rhodomontades of General von Herrt, the Governor of the city, the people felt that momentous events were at hand. As though the Germans were determined not to show the Belgians any but their most unlovely aspect, the Army of Occupation now mutinied. On November 7, tense excitement prevailed; on the tenth, tumult and anarchy broke loose. M. Lemonnier, the alderman, who had been acting-Burgomaster, had already managed to unlock the gates of his prison. Others, like M. Franck and M. Masson, both deputies, had secured their release. Thus the liberalism of Prince Max of Baden, the new German Chancellor, had manifested itself. On the tenth, "the reek of invasion," described by Brand Whitlock, had given place to the "reek of riot."

Between five and six thousand disbanded soldiers, preceded by a lorry piled with rifles, left the Gare du Nord about two o'clock, waving red banners and a French flag. The long procession filed slowly along the boulevards, making a pitiful attempt to simulate gaiety. Opposite the Bourse, they stopped a number of cars which had come from the direction of Ghent, rough-handled the officers who were in them, and wrenched off their epaulettes. The demonstrations were a repetition of the scenes that had occurred at Kiel. There

were manifestations at the Porte de Namur and the Place de Brouckère. At the Palais de la Nation the Red Flag was hoisted. At 5:30, in the Place de Brouckère, German naval marines arrived in cars, waving Belgian flags. One of them made a speech in French in praise of King Albert; it rang falsely in that chaos of defeat, to the bawling of drunken "Marseillaises."

The scum of the city slouched stealthily from dubious haunts, singly at first, then in small groups. Was Belgium, like Hungary, being swept towards a Government of Red Sailors? Newspaper kiosks were set ablaze. The fire brigade had to be called out to protect the General Post Office. Panic-stricken, the German Government capitulated.

It was said that the King would avenge himself up to the hilt. During his four years in office, von der Lancken had been forced to perform many humiliating duties. The worst of all was to come. On the night of the rioting, he hastened to Villalobar and implored him to send M. Franqui to the King without delay, so that he might beg him to "see that order was enforced and that the security of those Germans who had been unable to leave Belgian territory was guaranteed." Herr von der Lancken immediately produced the necessary passports.

The Marquis found M. Franqui at his house in the Avenue Louise. There was no time to be lost; the crowd had thrown open the prison of St. Gilles. Nevertheless, the great news had been received at the Maison du Peuple. Once again the serious and phlegmatic Belgian workers showed their solid worth. Though M.

Franqui was tempted by von der Lancken's plea that he should go to the King, the old soldier felt that it would be dangerous to leave his post of command at such a moment. He was hesitating when the door opened to admit M. Janson. "The very man!" he exclaimed. On the next day, November 11, "at 5 A.M. a German armoured car left Brussels for the front. Seated by Sr. Saura, the Spanish Consul, M. Janson, the delegate of the Belgians to the King of the Belgians, was dispassionately weighing up the overwhelming importance of his mission."

M. Janson's journey presented no difficulties. M. Franqui had done well to single him out from the surrounding crowd, for he was tact and delicacy personified. Kindly and upright, a man of great culture, he yet possessed a vein of shrewd scepticism and a great gift for seeing the picturesque and least obvious side of things. Such were the most striking attributes of this distinguished barrister of Brussels. But a closer analysis of his psychology would have revealed him to be profoundly pessimistic, with a deliberately dark outlook on men and events—in short, when he had carried out a task, something invariably impelled him to say: "What good will it do?" Of all the Ministers, M. Janson was the most liable to be stigmatized as a "Doubting Thomas," because he was as self-exacting and had as little faith in himself as the King. But no one was better fitted to plead a cause, transmit a delicate message with strict adherence to truth, unite the spirit and the letter, or make a lucid and unprejudiced exposition.

When he reached Ghent, M. Janson hastened to the Hôtel de Ville. The Burgomaster was in prison, but in his absence he transacted his business with a substitute who was entirely adequate. This was M. Anseele. When he learnt the object of M. Janson's and Sr. Saura's mission, the old Socialist leader exclaimed: "The King! I will go with you and take His Majesty the homage of the city of Ghent."

The Germans had left Ghent during the night, "after they had fired at random in the streets, evidently with the idea of forcing the inhabitants to remain indoors." Von der Lancken's car had been unable to enter the city. A great hubbub arose in the faubourg of Maria-kirke to the west of the town. The streets were thronged with crowds of workers, who had followed on the heels of the retreating German troops. On the preceding evening the Belgian officers, who knew that propositions for an Armistice were afoot, had given orders to cease fire.

It was mid-day when the two Belgian deputies and the Spanish Consul reached the Headquarters of Lieutenant-General Drubbel. The latter chanced to be a native of Ghent, having been born at Oostacker, a suburb of the city—the Flemish Lourdes. Although he was a soldier and a Catholic, he had known M. Anseele for many years. He invited the three statesmen to lunch, and sent a message to the King's headquarters. Drubbel was an excellent speaker in his own way; his sallies and picturesque language delighted Anseele. He spoke of his men. "We ought to go down on our knees to them," he said. M. Janson had a son, who had joined up dur-

ing the War, and who was an officer in the Infantry; he was stationed quite close to where they were. As they sat talking, the news of the Armistice came through. A telephone message was received that the King would expect the delegates at two-thirty. The General put his car and chauffeur at their disposal. At the stated hour, the immense red pile of Lophem came into sight. They drove between the hedges which formed part of the park, taking no heed of their surroundings. The car stopped. Major de Hennin de Boussu Walcourt opened the door of the Royal study.

M. Cooreman, the Catholic President of the Cabinet Council, was also present. The three men bowed respectfully. All three political parties were represented. The King, stooping a little, regarded them curiously, and shook hands with them. The two new-comers felt their throats constrict. They had not seen him since that stirring session on August 4, 1914. They had never before spoken to him. When M. Anseele had regained his self-control, he turned to M. Cooreman. The two had been antagonists on the Town Council of Ghent, from the time when M. Anseele had furiously denounced "the tight hand on the cash box," and had replied to what he called "insults" (which he pronounced "inshults"). Now the two old enemies shook hands warmly. It was a good beginning.

M. Janson was unequalled in the narration of a series of events; he omitted nothing, added nothing. He quietly related all that had taken place in Brussels, after which the King, with similar composure, summed up the various points that had been made. The plenipo-

tentiaries then requested to be allowed to discuss political matters, and M. Anseele outlined the programme of his Party: "Universal suffrage for men who have attained the age of twenty-one and who have resided in any town for six months; the repeal of Article 310 of the penal code (which refers to the right of association); the institution of a Flemish university, and, broadly speaking, a democratic policy and social reform." He spoke of the Sacred Union.[1] The King signified his approval of this outline. At the conclusion of the interview, he introduced the two delegates to the Queen, and returned to his study.

In the great salon at Lophem, beneath the wrought-iron chandelier, the frank agreement arrived at by these four sincere men laid the structure of the new Belgian Government. The King listened to Anseele, and the resonant voice of the old Red leader had seemed to swell into that of a crowd—the vast crowd of poor and needy, the weavers, toilers and workers, who, in a highly-mechanized era, operated looms, hewed coal, baked bricks, blew glass, and loaded the holds of ships. Through the mouth of their prophet, they said to the King: "We love and revere you. We are ready to serve you; we know that you wish us well, and we place our trust in you." M. Janson tells us that Anseele's words were deferential yet stirring. What a contrast to the restrained Parisian oratory of the learned man of law! Anseele's language was colourful and racy, challenging

---

[1] At the outbreak of War, all three political parties and their adherents, rich and poor, united in the service of Belgium. This was the Sacred Union.

and full-blooded, delivered with that appalling Ghent-
ish sibilance which is more tenacious than the accent of
Marseilles. And those who were swayed by his eloquence came from the ranks of his most stubborn political opponents.

During the days which followed, the King and the
statesmen mutually agreed that the speech on the re-
opening of the Chamber should be made on the sixteenth. The formation of a new Government would
be announced. It would be elected by universal suffrage. The foundation of a Flemish University was
also promised. All M. Franqui's friends were at Lophem, but he himself was absent. So too was M. Vandervelde, though he remarked later, when he heard of the
great decision: "I am overjoyed. I expected no less
from the King's breadth of vision."

It was possible to constitute a Ministry within a very
short time. M. de Broqueville had been sounded and
had agreed to take office, as had M. Renkin who, according to the rumours at Le Havre, was his most deadly
rival. Only one of the new Cabinet had any doubts.
This was Baron Ruzette, a senator of Bruges and a re-
lation of M. van Caloen. The fabric that had been
spun in his cousin's château disquieted him in more
than one respect, and he made his consent subject to
that of M. de Broqueville. But one after another all
doubts dissolved into thin air, and M. Léon Delacroix,
the President, a devout churchman, and the great Beernaert's favourite pupil, inspired confidence amongst the
Catholic element. There could not have been a better
President for a triple coalition where the interests of

Socialists, Liberals, and Catholics were equally served. This sincere co-operation in the Sacred Union was soon to receive the approval of the people.

Only one detail had been overlooked in this great symphony. During the War, in the hours of uncertainty at Le Havre, M. de Broqueville had entrusted a committee which consisted of M. de Jonghe, the Socialist barrister, Auguste Dewinne, the journalist and an old militant Socialist, and Fernand Neuray, the famous journalist, a Catholic and Nationalist, with the drawing up of a detailed scheme for electoral reform. They had evolved a formula for universal suffrage for men at the age of twenty-five, the heads of households to be entitled to two votes. M. Vandervelde had signified his approval, as had M. de Broqueville. This scheme, although it was very progressive, reassured the Catholics, and was well in line with the Masson amendment of 1913, that amendment which had put an end to the strike by promising "a more favourable electoral system." M. Cooreman could not, or dared not, recall this proposed reform. M. de Broqueville was absent, and was only called upon when the appointments had been made. No one but M. Vandervelde remembered it, but he took malicious satisfaction, seemingly, in concealing his knowledge.

The general agreement at Lophem was nothing more than what is known in England as a "gentlemen's agreement." Although everything had been straightforward, it was one day to appear underhand and equivocal. The Franqui Committee deserved full consideration

from Belgium for the immense services it had rendered; it had helped to maintain order, and had gathered round it the great living forces of the nation. Yet it was ultimately to be treated as a Soviet of lawyers. M. Vandervelde had scarcely taken part in any of these conferences, yet he was to be cited as the source of their inspiration. The Brussels Committee, the château in Flanders—both these were to take on a clandestine aspect. Incidentally, insufficient publicity had been given to the discussion. There were tentative requests for more light. Von der Lancken's panic and the Marquis of Villalobar's anxiety had first set the ball rolling, and a rumour was spread that there had been a deliberate attempt to terrorize the King.

It was only a step further from this to positive belief in a conspiracy: the conspiracy of Lophem. However inclusive a private conference may be, it always has the appearance of secret diplomacy. Even the King's caution was regarded as audacity. On November 12, he had ordered M. Ingenbleek to go to the Bishop of Ghent: "Ask him what he really thinks. He is a clever man, and close to the people. For many years he was a priest in the parish of St. Jean Baptiste, the most populous district of the town. . . ." On the whole, the Bishop had agreed with M. Anseele. But Mgr. Waffelaert, the Bishop of Bruges, held other views, and had not been consulted. Link by link, a chain of lying rumours was forged round Lophem. The most moderate of these ran: "What a pity! It only shows that a King who is a hero in war-time may be a coward in politics. It only took a few Socialists and unscrupulous

lawyers to turn his head completely . . . with the help of Ingenbleek, his evil genius. . . ."

It should always be remembered that the King was a pessimist and a sceptic. He belonged to that category of men whose brains do not function properly unless their minds are at rest. Sycophants, of course, now assured him that he had emerged greater than ever from the Lophem conference. He never listened to them. Others insinuated that he had blundered badly, that he had been afraid. And to these he listened with rage in his heart, until 1934, until the day of his death.

The King's feelings were divided between joy of victory and disappointment at not being able to make the most of his day of triumph by re-entering Brussels at the point of the sword. All the omens seemed to foretell that the château's days of glory were drawing to an end. It will never be known whether the King loved this countryside of Bruges, this tiny village of Lophem to which chance had brought him, and whose name, later on, was to cause him such pangs of agony.

The Queen visited the abbey, and once more exercised her predilection for the Benedictine life—a predilection she had inherited. But Albert was the true contemplative. None of the people of Bruges or Lophem, peasant, landowner or priest, was made the recipient of his confidence. He was a dreamer; an athlete who scoured the country on foot or on horseback, who never shot a pheasant, but who studied plant life and the migrations of birds. Often, before giving an order, he would bury himself in thought as if he

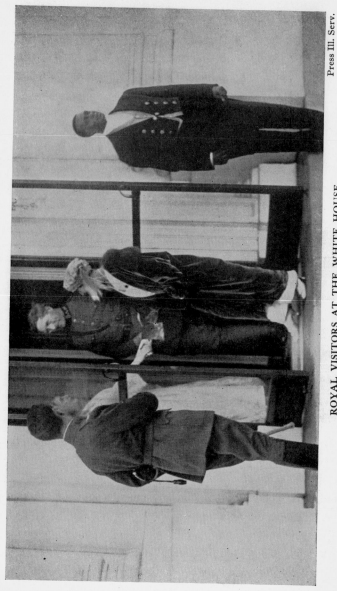

ROYAL VISITORS AT THE WHITE HOUSE

were praying. One morning, the procession formed up
for the Joyous Entry into Ghent. . . . Statesmen came
and went. M. Pierre and Van Dyck fastened trunks
and sorted out silver. The Queen's riding-boots were
no longer to be seen—those boots which Van Dyck pol-
ished, and which were so much admired by all the children of the house. They were so tiny that they might
have been worn by an elf.

On that last Sunday at Lophem, in order to set a
good example, the King and the Duke of Brabant went
once more to eleven o'clock Mass in the parish church.
As they came out, the peasants devoured them with
their eyes, speechless, sealed up in their own intense
shyness. The King looked at them, as they looked at
him, in silence, and they found mutual cause for admiration. Thirteen years later, in 1931, the King said
to me: "You remember Lophem. . . ." There was a
long pause, and then he added, stressing every word:
"I have been treated as a coward or a fool or both, for
the decisions that I made there in full awareness of all
the facts and of my own free will. I want you to know
that what I did at Lophem, I did of my own accord,
actuated by none but myself. This may enlighten you
later on, in your career as a journalist. . . ."

The great day of departure arrived. The King, the
Queen and the Princes got into the car. The van
Caloen children were lined up on the steps, their parents in the centre, waving their hands. The cars moved
slowly off. The Princess leaned out of the window,
clutching her pet rabbit, and made him wave "Good-
bye, good-bye," with his front paws.

It had been the King's wish that the Entry into Brussels should take the same order as in 1909, and that it should start from Laeken. Before he re-entered his capital, he re-entered his home. It was mid-day when the cars drove through the old quarter of Brussels and, avoiding the town, reached the Palace. Four years had passed. The gendarmes presented arms. Bugles sounded in the meadows. At the end of the avenue the Palace came into sight once more. The gravel crunched beneath the wheels. The King gazed hungrily at his beautiful park, the trees that had sprung up, the rhododendrons that had grown. But it was he himself who had grown most of all.

All the servants, in scarlet livery, were drawn up in the great hall. There are some dramas whose *dénouements* are too beautiful to be true, too neatly dovetailed to be lifelike. This was just such an ending, yet it was both beautiful and true. The King and Queen had a word for every one of their old servants, whom they shook by the hand and questioned affectionately about their families and well-being. A magnificent lunch was served in the Salon des Maréchaux. The officers of the suite, nearly all of whom had only recently been appointed, saw for the first time this royal splendour which so far removed them from the tiny court of La Panne and the country court of Lophem.

At two o'clock the horses were brought round. The King was helped into the saddle by Henriette, the groom who had performed the same office for him on the day of his coronation.

CHAPTER XI

POST-WAR

THE Entry into Bruges had been joyful. The Entry into Ghent had been triumphal. The Entry into Brussels was, as it should have been, an apotheosis.

The escort at Bruges had been the 1st Regiment of Guides, who had recently covered themselves with glory at Burkel, between Bruges and Ghent, recalling the golden age of cavalry charges. For the last time the Belgian troops appeared in Ghent on the very day of the Armistice, driving the enemy out of the city at the point of the bayonet. But in Brussels, on November 22, when the gendarmes, with their black peaked caps, appeared at the Porte de Flandre—when the gigantic figure of the King on a white horse, between the Queen and the Duke of Brabant, came into sight—the people rubbed their eyes and wondered if what they saw were real.

The vanished days of August 4, 1914, and of King Albert's first Joyous Entry into Brussels in December, 1909, seemed insignificant and infinitely far off in the presence of this almost dreamlike procession. The newspapers spoke of the King's face as being "radiant," but they were wrong; for at such moments the King never smiled. The overpowering homage of the whole nation rose up to him, and he took deep breaths of its heavenly incense. But his face never lost its lines of

care, and his proud humility never suffered a smile of joy to soften his stern features. He assumed an expressionless mask, lest he should appear arrogant. But beneath his non-committal exterior, his spirit was uplifted. The Queen, who was in grey, was exultant. The Princes were smiling. The escort thrilled with excitement. So it had been at Antwerp, where the strong wind from the Scheldt had swelled the standards, and at Malines, where the Cardinal, erect at the entrance to St. Rombaut, looked as though he had descended from one of his own stained-glass windows.

The entry of the Belgian troops into Brussels was picturesque to a degree. Until then the task of the military authorities had consisted far less in driving the retreating German troops before them than in keeping back their own advance guard, desperately anxious to reach the capital. The victorious infantry, no longer under strict military discipline, had found it hardest of all to break through the cordon of Belgian cavalry which barred their way. Meanwhile, in Brussels the crowd was stamping its feet with impatience.

Since November 12, when German officers and soldiers were still firing revolver shots at each other round the Gare du Nord, another and then another Belgian soldier had appeared near the Bourse, in uniform and unarmed. They had smuggled themselves into the capital. With the recklessness of youth, one of them had cycled past the German column all the way from Ghent. As he rode by, hundreds of soldiers in field-grey, dragging themselves along, were roused by his bell, and greeted him with a gloomy: "Morgen . . . Kam-

erad. . . ." In the villages he caught sight of strange-looking men dressed as priests. They were fleeing Germans, fearful of reprisals; glimpses of their boots could be seen beneath their soutanes. When he reached the boulevards, our daring Belgian soldier was almost hugged to death by the delirious throng. Above the clamour, pathetic appeals were heard: "Have you any news of so-and-so? He was in the army too. . . ." Perhaps he and so-and-so had been friends. . . . Other voices said warningly: "Look out! Don't go that way! They are still firing at one another."

And now, in the Marolles, the jubilant denizens of the Rue Haute and the Place de Jeu de Balle celebrated a witches' sabbath. Flags with triumphal inscriptions were stretched across the thronged streets. A mock funeral of the Kaiser was held, of course. The simulation of the solemn burial of their enemies, complete with hearse and hymn-singing, is one of the diversions dearest to the Marollian heart. Hoodlums armed themselves with scissors and shears, and for several days those unfortunate women who had sold themselves to the Germans were mauled, punched black and blue and sheared like sheep going to the slaughter. (In Ghent, infuriated workmen had flung buckets of petrol over the houses of traitors and set them ablaze like torches.)

Flags appeared everywhere as if by magic; and portraits of the King, the Queen, and the Royal children were proudly displayed. I knew some girls who for two years had concealed a photograph of Princess Marie-José, taken in her First Communion dress outside the chapel at La Panne. They had cleverly hidden the tiny

picture under another. When the Germans at length left their house, they rushed to the album and put the photograph of the Princess on the front page. During these first days, seven million Belgians made gestures of this sort; and the German soldiers, bowed down beneath their misery, murmured, as they passed the victorious people: "Morgen . . . Kamerad. . . ."

The Court settled down, for the time being, in the Palace of Brussels and the Palace of Flanders. Laeken, with its orchid houses, library, gardens, and its roomy study full of documents and souvenirs, was being put in order, and would at last become the kingdom of flowers and books that the King had so richly deserved. One night a strange wooden contraption arrived there in sections. It was the bungalow from La Panne, where the Queen had spent so many hours with her books. It was set up at Laeken, complete with its blue cushions and blue hangings.

After Versailles, all the continental countries were plunged into a financial nightmare. Belgium suffered a nationalist nightmare as well.

Flemish Activists during the War had laid the structure first of a university, then of a State; but their attempts had ended in fiasco. The Flemish question, however, had still to be settled and a minimum of its claims to be recognized; a university at Ghent; Flemish to be the language of the administration, the law and education; the Army to be recruited regionally; in short, the beginnings of federation into an integral State. It was within the scope of the Constitution to carry out these

reforms, and therefore they could be effected peacefully. Thus the King was able to entertain the idea of them without disfavour. They might, however, prove a serious danger to the moral unity of the country.

The entire population of Flanders, with the exception of the Fransquillon minorities, now demanded a Flemish university at Ghent. This was a collective blunder because it looked like a resurrection of Activist misdemeanours. Whether they wanted to or not, the Flamingants appeared in the light of traitors, the descendants of traitors. The majority of them were worthy and respectable citizens; but the riff-raff also ranged themselves under the common standard.

Flemish agitators began to stir up trouble. Most of the Activist leaders had been sentenced by default. A few of them had remained in the country, however. Public meetings seethed with hatred. There was not a single act of violence; but the Activist leaders took advantage of the fear that a judicial sentence invariably inspires in the peasant mind, and began to sow the seeds of trouble in every village.

Only one member of the Council of Flanders—of those who had actually been condemned to death—remained in the country. This was Auguste Borms, a Professor at the Royal Lycée of Antwerp. I saw him on several occasions at meetings and Flemish demonstrations. No one could have been better suited to play the part of figurehead in a serious movement. He was a coarse-looking, commonplace, red-bearded man; fairly well informed; a devout Catholic, or calling himself so; married; and the author of sob-stuff articles about his

"darling little wife";—just the kind of puffed-up crea-
ture, in fact, to make an admirable totem. Had he had
brains, Borms might have become a second Hitler. But
he had none; he appeared lacking even in animal intelligence. The Germans had won him over by flattery,
and had made him Minister for War of the State of
Flanders. Borms, *per se,* was so ludicrous that the
Judges felt he would have done them a favour had he
bolted like the rest. But in 1918, Borms had shaved off
his red beard, and had lain hidden in Brussels. When
discovered, he was condemned to death, reprieved, and
imprisoned in Louvain. He spent ten years in a cell,
well fed and well treated; and during those ten years
his fame grew like a snowball rolling down hill.

The Belgian State could easily have disposed of the
Borms affair by releasing him. Once liberated, the
grotesque Auguste would have become harmless. But
at the same time this would have been a premature par-
don, an insult to the soldiers of the Yser; and chauvinist
feeling would have been outraged. In the meantime,
Borms became the Martyr of Flanders, a bugbear that
was raised to terrify the "Brussels crowd" and the inhabitants of "official Belgium." Once more the yellow
and black flags appeared as if by magic in every village
in Flanders, bearing the device of the seagull, the wailing harbinger of the storm—the seagull whom the Flemish unfortunately prefer to Minerva's owl when things
go wrong. People who had nothing in common with
Activism associated with those who were most deeply
involved. As had been the case in the *affaire Dreyfus,*
the country was divided on a question of right.

The Flemish are turbulent by nature. They now became extraordinarily touchy, and it seemed as though Civil War were imminent. Plaster statuettes of Borms and the "Idealists" were hawked about. *Amnesty* was the watchword of the day, and Borms was proclaimed uncrowned King of Flanders. In his prison cell, Auguste inhaled the pothouse incense that rose up to him.

The cause of this emotional unrest among the Flemings was not, of course, incomprehensible. The Activists called their party the *Frontpartij*—and the name was well chosen. The region nearest to the German trenches had suffered absolute martyrdom during the four years' inferno of shelling from both sides, and was a howling waste. Once again, as so often in the past, Flanders, the battleground of Europe, was going to shoulder pickaxe and spade. But this time the earth had not merely been trampled over; it had been flung into chaotic heaps. The farmers had come back one by one, looking for what had once been their meadows; they lived in dug-outs and stumbled across forgotten shells that exploded without warning.

The administration at Brussels was slowly straightening out the confusion. Reconstruction Committees were formed, and this led to trouble. The Flemish grew angry. Misfortune was invariably visited on their heads, they complained; the Walloons and the people of Brussels were always well out of the range of disaster. They, the Flemish, had supplied the majority of troops in the trenches; they had been through the horrors of l'Etape; they had been treated with derision by the rich

Fransquillon landowners; and now, to crown all, it was amongst their ranks that Activists and traitors were being sought.

The King made a thorough tour of inspection through suffering Flanders. He had spent four years in this flat country, whose every spire he knew; and he was practically the only native statesman of Brussels who had made a searching study of Flemish and the *Thiois* dialects. As he well knew, also, neither the man in the street nor the politicians believed in the reality of Flemish Nationalism. But he was certain that Belgium, under a democratic régime, would have to satisfy the Flamingant demands up to the hilt. And every time the politicians made a new concession to the Flamingants, they declared it was the last. Albert's natural pessimism served him well, in those days.

Meanwhile, for two years, the War area looked like a stony waste or a lunar plain haunted by strange apparitions. The Government had made the mistake of recruiting Anamite labour for the work of reconstruction. The native workmen went from ruined village to ruined village and lived on what they could loot. The returned peasants banded themselves together, wandered over the country, and saw red if they were interfered with. Many went out by twos and threes with their priest at night, to exhume their dead from the State cemeteries and carry them back to their village churchyards. These funeral cortèges were often to be seen by moonlight, strangely symbolic of the resurrection of downtrodden Flanders—a sorrowful resurrec-

tion overcast by visions of graves, spectres and midnight prayers.

At length, by constitutional process, the Flemish claims were established, in terms Albert had agreed to at Lophem. He now toured the country again, accompanied by one of his Ministers, M. Ruzette, who had been born at Ypres, and was a Senator from Bruges. At the end of a day's excursion, they would sleep in Ostend. The Royal Villa was not in very good repair; when the King showed the Minister to his room, he noticed that the plug of the bath was missing and stopped it up himself with a piece of cork.

Everything simmered down as soon as the new Flemish régime was established. The process, however, entailed some difficulty, because bourgeois opinion, unaccustomed to Flamingant ideas, disputed the ground inch by inch. Whenever the question of Flanders was raised in the Chamber a storm broke loose. The Flemish deputies assumed the air of martyrs: minority parties, when they find their strength increasing, customarily make the most of their wrongs to the exclusion of other business. Several deputies from the *Frontpartij* had been elected, and these "seagull" members invariably spoke in funereal language and heart-rending tones—the mournful and denunciatory eloquence of Redemptorist Fathers.

Finally, in 1920, the Government released Dr. Borms, and the uncrowned King of Flanders was to be met at all public manifestations. One freezing January morning in Antwerp, I saw him being carried shoulder-high amidst tense excitement. His beard had grown again,

and he gazed vacantly around him. By a poignant paradox, the crowd was being kept back by the soldiers of
the Yser, covered with medals, who thrust themselves
between the Septembrists and the traitor to his country,
the Minister for War of the Council of Flanders. I
suppose such scenes as these must have resembled those
which took place in Petrograd and Moscow. Under the
lowering sky, Flanders is capable of equally disastrous
folly, equally catastrophic eruptions. At that time its
fate hung by a thread, for, had Europe given any signs
of ill-feeling, the Borms clan would have rent the multi-
coloured coat of Flanders in two and there would have
been civil war as there was in Ireland.

I remember seeing the King during this time in his
study in Brussels. He was pessimistic as usual, but in
no way disturbed. In his opinion, this outbreak was
like a rash that would fade, and he believed that the
Flemish were only concentrating their anger on those
who by virtue of their positions had caused them the
bitterest humiliation. The guiltiest parties in this respect were the Law and the Army.

Impelled by their deep-rooted mysticism, Flamingants of every shade of feeling organized a yearly pil-
grimage to the Yser. In the vast plain of Dixmude, at
the foot of a futuristic Calvary, there would sometimes be
as many as fifty thousand of them grouped behind standards that billowed majestically in the wind from the
sea. A priest said Mass. Speakers, monks and laymen,
succeeded one another on the platform, so that sacred
and profane rubbed shoulders. Disabled men accompanied Dr. Borms, prayers alternated with insults, and

imprecations against Belgium mingled with the deep murmur of the reeds of the Yser, where so many men of Flanders had fallen in defence of their King and United Belgium.

Just as a conflagration leaps up, darts forth licking tongues of flame and then dies down for want of fuel, so Frontism or Flemish Nationalism was suddenly extinguished. Borms, having been set at liberty, fell into oblivion within a year. The Savonarolas of the presbyteries calmed down when the Flemish laws had been voted. In 1932, Frontism was defeated at the polls. Its most vehement exponents accepted office, and, desirous of retaining it, turned conservative now that they had something to conserve.

The wisdom of the King, which had incessantly manifested itself throughout the long drama, was to receive its crowning reward. Had he died in 1929 or 1930, he would have left behind him a country rent and torn by party factions. Providence allowed him to live long enough to see unity restored, and the whirlwind, the notorious Flemish whirlwind, subside. National unity, which had momentarily hung in the balance, had been saved by monarchic unity. The Flemish affair was to expire like the Alsatian affair, and for the same reason: lack of combustible matter. The Flemish extremists had caused the King exactly the same sort of worry that the French extremists had caused the French Government. The dispute was not serious if the underlying motives were understood—above all, if no offensive blunder were committed. To-day the *Frontpartij* is divided

amongst itself, and Belgium is at peace because King
Albert never lost his sense of proportion.

Deeply impressed by the virtues and rugged qualities
of his people, King Albert knew every twist and turn of
their unique and heroic character. He even *breathed*
Belgium, and so sure was his intuition that his ministers
left in amazement after an interview with him. "He is
the only man who really knows the country," they said.

He soon realized which of his cousins of other countries was near to, or distant from, the hearts of the people, and he felt an affection full of pride for the Prince
of Wales and King Boris of Bulgaria. They were both
true sons of his race, royal in spirit, able to divine in a
flash what was passing in the minds of their subjects.
It is impossible to tell to what party such men belong.
Was Albert I Catholic, Socialist or Liberal? No one
knows, and in all probability he himself did not know.
He was very devout, very socialistic and very broad-
minded, and may well have been the ideal of men be-
longing to all three parties. However that may be, he
knew them surprisingly well. Gone was the time when
he asked his old Ministers for advice. He himself appointed them; in 1911, of his own accord, and against
the advice of the leaders of the Right Wing, he had
selected M. de Broqueville, the doyen of them all.

Fernand Neuray wrote that Albert I was every inch
a King. He had become so by identifying himself
wholly with his country. I have often said to his
friends: "The King adored machinery—he might have
become a great engineer. He knew the Congo through

and through—he would have made a great Colonial administrator. He was a splendid officer—he could have been a great teacher at the Ecole de Guerre." To which one and all replied in effect: "You are wrong. He was purely a King, just as a monk is a monk, and a soldier a soldier. His position as King had absorbed all his faculties to such an extent that Kingship became second nature to him. The King and his Kingship were one and indivisible."

The King may have complained of having to be King. But many men of mark are wont to say of their career: "What a profession!" Albert I used to repeat: "I shall soon abdicate. Leopold is old enough to succeed me. My wife and I will go to Haslykorn, and in that corner of Switzerland I shall live happily amidst my books and the mountains. Once a priest has retired, he should not go on living in his former parish."

In his heart of hearts, however, these words meant nothing. If he himself were not attached to his Kingship, that Kingship was to be attached to him forever. Had a day dawned when he, who so often found it boring to be a King, had found himself King no longer, he would have died of boredom. And it was the same, too, with his nationalism. In his moody moments, he would say in his deep voice: "I will do this and that. Of course, the Belgians won't understand, and will tear everything to pieces with criticism"; and the Queen would laughingly reprove him. Yet by the sole reason of duty well and truly done, he was the most Belgian of all the Belgians.

CHAPTER XII

THE KING AND HIS REIGN

PICTURE King Albert as he appeared towards the end, in the prime of life. He was a colossus. In this Saxe-Coburg Prince, with the blood of Orléans and Sigmaringen in his veins, slow and precise of speech, we recognize the heir to a race inured to laborious and conscientious thinking. He was an athlete, tanned by his climbing expeditions, his journeys by car and 'plane; a scholar and soldier, driven by his royal rank into the sphere of politics.

A first encounter with him was an intimidating and somewhat embarrassing experience. But as soon as the ball was set rolling, his visitor would become aware of an extraordinarily lucid mind which selected words as if each one had been carefully weighed and considered. It was almost as though he consulted Littré for every sentence. And it is true that every word Albert used was so exactly right, his construction so flawless, the turn of phrase so happy, that one forgot the Viennese accent—his polyglot heritage—and only remembered the precision with which he expressed the truth. Sometimes he would smile a little hesitatingly, and this trace of shyness was entirely in keeping with his character.

It was not until late in life that the King, with his dynamic energy and keen and sensitive mind, derived

benefit from his education. He had been treated like
a mere subaltern in his youth, and had been regarded
as the fifth spoke in the chariot-wheel of the Monarchy,
the younger son of a younger branch, until he had
reached man's estate. There was a time when he
thought that every man of mature years who was presented to him must possess an ability greater than his
own. Since then an uneasy reserve, a dread of having
said too much,—or if he said too little, of seeming ignorant,—had developed in the mind of this keen observer,
this voracious reader.

On top of this, he had been educated by ill-chosen
tutors, and had soon realized that although he spoke
four languages he knew none of them well. When he
was much older, at the age of twenty-five, he set himself
to study them, as he did many other subjects. His
speech was that of a scholar who had long remained in
an arrested state of development. The scholar Prince
had taught himself like a penniless student by poring
over the text-books of his more fortunate friends. Unlike his uncles and cousins of Orléans, he had never
mingled, as a young man, in literary circles—had never
met brilliant women, writers and artists. "We Coburgs
are formed late in life," he would say. The fact is, no
one had taken the trouble to form his mind; and late
in life it was he who formed it himself.

It was useless to recommend him a book or a new
review—he would invariably have read it. His literary
interests ranged from Paul Valéry's poems to Huxley's
essays, from the parliamentary history of Belgium to
works on the flora and fauna of the Congo. When he

came across a superficial or slipshod book, he would grimace silently and lay it aside.

Although he was careless in his dress except when he was in uniform, as I have said before, Albert was very particular as to the arrangement of his documents and files. Each had to be in its right place. "Twenty years ago," he once remarked, "I wrote a book about the problem of transport in the Congo. I had kept all my sketches, maps and calculations. I lent the MS. to a friend. War broke out, and he has never returned my work." Thoughtlessness of this kind threw him into a cold rage.

When he folded or rolled up a map, he would say: "I must be careful not to crease it." Before his departure to the Great African Lakes, he learned by heart the native names of every stage on his journey, down to those of the tiniest village. An old Colonial, amazed by this knowledge, exclaimed: "Your Majesty has been here before!" "No; but my maps are excellent," said the King quietly.

The maps were excellent. . . . The work was excellent. . . . An indefatigable worker, the King had a master craftsman's passion for perfection. He would often say with a sigh: "Leopold II knew how to write. I wish I resembled him. . . ." He never wrote for the sake of writing. Bent over his blotting-pad, he found correspondence an arduous task. He had all the difficulty in the world in finding the right word on paper, although it came to him so readily when he talked. He would make four or five fresh starts; and when he had finished, his relentless spirit of criticism

would drive him to re-write it entirely. He would
scratch out dozens of words. A thick-handled pen-knife
always lay on his table, and no sooner had the ink dried
than he would erase one word and substitute another.
He made alterations of this kind in his letters, drafts
of speeches and even in the inscriptions he wrote on
his photographs for his aides-de-camp.

Sometimes, tired of his monkish toil, he would sum-
mon his secretary and read aloud what he had written.
As he read, he would see that the phrasing was clumsy,
the construction heavy. "Doesn't it strike you as being
rather *pappich?*" he would ask.

Albert's distaste for writing would have been a great
loss had he been able to leave any manuscripts behind
him. But had he written any memoirs or notes of advice to the Government, they would undoubtedly have
been destroyed. Those written by Leopold I and Leopold II were burnt: only the first Queen, Louise-Marie,
has left letters. Leopold II jotted down notes for his
nephew's guidance, and added: "Burn them all." The
documents of the Court of Belgium seem doomed not
to remain extant.

The King brought his intellectual honesty to bear
on every aspect of political life. He had few friends
outside his own household. Was it because of his innate mistrust? Life had intensified his shyness. We
know that he appreciated the work of his loyal subjects, and that his gratitude was as great as his distrust,
but his transparent candour laid him open to much
suffering. How often did he say: "So-and-so promised

me his support. I believed him; but he has not kept his word." He was never able to understand the weaknesses, inconsistencies and double-dealings of politicians. He himself always kept his promises, or never made any. Why, then, when a Minister made a promise to the King, did he not keep it? This was one of the bitternesses of his life.

He never gave his trust twice. Louis-Philippe, his grandfather, loved to trip up his deputies, says Pierre de la Gorce. Anything of this sort filled Albert with loathing. A soldier gives his opinion and sticks to it. With an inherent love for peace and solitude, he would let unimportant matters slide, and say: "What's the use?" He was perfectly indifferent to flattery, and sarcastic to flatterers. He only lost his temper when he was reproached for not intervening or for not making up his mind. When complimented on his erudition, he would reply: "Oh, the Kings of to-day have plenty of time for reading." There was the same underlying bitterness when he referred to the niggardly sums that were doled out to him: "What a lot of wonderful things I might do." These words were incessantly on his lips.

He had a caustic wit, full of unexpected flashes. He rarely lost control of himself, but his friends occasionally saw him in appalling rages. These were provoked by his consciousness that some move or other in international politics had a personal significance for him. The German Ultimatum of August 4, 1914, was to him an affair of honour to be thrashed out between the Hohenzollern and himself. Wilhelm II had made many fine speeches to him, and had been given a wonderful re-

ception in Brussels. This made the Ultimatum a stab
in the back. When the King was a prey to these fits
of rage, his lower lip would quiver in a curious manner.

No one knows by what slow steps his mind at length
built up his ultimate monarchic doctrine. I have often
asked his friends what he thought about democracy, the
Flemish question, materialism, and monarchy in general. They all told me that I must not look for a rigid
code, a tabulated summary of knowledge, or a declara-
tion of faith. He left neither memoirs nor confessions,
nor a decalogue behind him, and it is impossible to gain
a complete insight into his thoughts from isolated words
and actions. To understand him, we must take a broad
view of his reign. Although his mind was as candid
in 1934 as in 1914, it had matured by contact with men
and events. His integrity was static; his opinions never
were. He had too much intellectual pride to hold hard
and fast views.

It would be interesting to know whether at any stage
in his life-work he was the avowed disciple of Taine or
Machiavelli, Maurras or Karl Marx. He most certainly
read them, but he was never exclusively influenced by
any one of them, either in sociology or political science.
The Stuarts had their scholars, the Hohenstaufens their
jurists. The Bourbons left behind them majestic for-
mulae which were extended by each succeeding generation, just as fresh treaties are made to confirm existing
treaties. It would appear as if, from the testament of
Louis XIV to that of the Duke of Alençon, the Bourbons had put their whole minds to consolidating by
new documents what the old had already established.

In these records we see them justifying their right to reign, setting forth their claims and exalting themselves to the position of political doctrinaires. The King of the Belgians never laid down any such dicta.

Let us go deeper into his psychology. It almost seems as if, during those last years, no other mind had the power to influence his. It was often asked: "Who is influencing the King?" We should like to know whether the King of the Belgians had any favourites amongst his Ministers. There were a few whom he trusted, though he rarely praised them. It is said that he showed marked preference for M. Vandervelde. This is obviously untrue, since in spite of his great admiration for the mentality and wide knowledge of the Socialist Minister, he ignored him whenever he felt it expedient, just as he would ignore a Catholic or a Liberal. I have been shown numbers of letters signed with a firm and decided *"A"*; one and all are written in an even hand without erasures, and every down-stroke has been traced with the same care and precision. They invariably begin: "My dear Minister" or "My dear Prime Minister," and are signed: "Your affectionate Albert." The style is classic in its perfection, the sentences are exquisitely balanced, show an extraordinary feeling for the *mot juste,* and convey in full the dignity of the writer. He hardly ever writes "I wish," but very often "I believe" and never "I am certain." Yet when the day came for a Minister to receive his *congé,* he was given an audience . . . and all was over.

Did his coldness contain an element of bitterness against Parliamentary mechanism? I am tempted to be-

lieve so. The Belgian Constitution defines the power of
the Monarch in a singular way. Each Party designates
those of their members from whom he may select his
Ministers. When Albert's Ministers had given up
office, he took no further interest in them. He often
esteemed, sometimes admired, the colleagues who were
temporarily imposed on him. He had great faith in a
few. To one of the most distinguished of them he remarked: "You, at any rate, have always told me the
truth." This, one might think, was a supreme compliment which should have raised the Minister to a
pinnacle and made him the recipient of a host of small
favours. It did not do so; the Minister in question was
treated all his life with the same official courtesy and
tact as the rest.

The Premier alone, the closest to his Royal master,
was admitted with more intimacy into the daily round.
If he were ill, he might telephone his business to the
King. If the matter were urgent, he might hasten to
Laeken or, in case of need, to Ciergnon, where he would
find the King in the woods, dressed as a day-labourer,
planting or measuring oak-trees. Or he might find him
buried in books and papers, making maps and sketches,
in the interval between two excursions on his motor-
cycle. If the Premier stayed at Ciergnon, the Princes
moved on to another floor and gave up their room to
the distinguished visitor. It was a large, bare apartment.

If any Minister, whether he were in office or not,
suffered a bereavement, fell ill or was the victim of an
accident, the King instantly showed that solicitude of

which he was so chary in other circumstances. A
former President of the Chamber, who had broken his
arm, received a charming letter. I asked him if he were
often honoured in this way. "No," he said. "We never
see each other." The King treated his elderly statesmen with the special courtesy due to their years, and
the younger men with a lighter touch more suited to
their age. Each one might believe that he was more
favoured than the rest, but not one of them could flatter
himself that he had been admitted for all time into the
circle of the King's intimate friends. On the other
hand, if a political crisis arose, he would send for the
leaders of all three parties—even for those from whom
he knew he would learn nothing. Thus no jealousy
was occasioned; and the King treated them all alike,
with ironic indifference or guarded admiration. One
feels that his attitude to his Ministers was that of a master to his class. The types remain the same, though the
individuals change; and it is incumbent on him to de-
vote himself entirely to this class, about which he has
no illusions.

The great flaw in this system was, of course, that
Albert had many mediocre Ministers; and these had to
be treated with the same stereotyped courtesy and official consideration as the rest. The Ministry of the King
was synonymous with the confidence of the King, so
that any Minister in office could count on his unfailing
support. Only to his own intimate friends could he
vent his rage against them, stigmatize them as preten-
tious and absurd fools whom he himself could never
dismiss, although he realized to the full their incapacity.

THE ROYAL FAMILY ON HOLIDAY AT ST. MORITZ

He suffered all the more acutely because he was aware
what the intelligent public thought of his incompetent
Ministers; and he surmised the underlying accusation:
that the King was weak, that he dared not act, that he
allowed his Ministers to be foisted on him without exer-
cising any personal choice. He imagined a veiled reproach behind the admiration of the crowd on ceremonial occasions, and his mind, so prone to suspicion,
made him believe that one and all were disparaging
him. Near-sighted though he was, he would at once
distinguish the handful of spectators who had omitted
to applaud him. From his self-chosen pedestal the
King thought he could reckon up his paltry detractors,
his enemies and his narrow-minded critics. He came
to the conclusion that the Belgians are incorrigible—
that their tiresome habit of choral demonstrations, of
breaking into "Brabançonnes" on every occasion, of
speechifying and presenting medals, is ineradicable.
All this made him withdraw still deeper into himself.
The public believed that he was a misanthrope; and for
once the public was right.

The Peace that the King had so ardently desired for
the sake of his country came too swiftly in the wake of
glory. Belgium had already experienced her first dis-
illusionment at Versailles. Crowned with the laurels
of victory, the Belgian delegates hastened thither as if
they were going to a Pantheon of Right and Justice.
The Pantheon turned out to be a hornets' nest. Not
only did President Wilson and Lloyd George seem reluctant to listen to the Belgians—they soon forgot Bel-

gium. There was so much to be done. Clémenceau
was gaily hacking up the Austro-Hungarian Empire.
President Wilson and Lloyd George had fixed the seat
of the League of Nations at Geneva. This decision had
caused bitter disappointment in Brussels, for so strong
had been the illusion of a nation saturated in heroism
that it had been taken for granted that the capital of
Peace would be the capital of Justice. However logical
this assumption was, the choice of Brussels would have
been inexpedient. The Belgian delegates met with
failure after failure. At length M. Hymans, the leading delegate, went to Brussels and begged the King to
intervene.

The King's mission to Geneva must have imposed a
further stratum of scepticism on his nature. Solemnly
he pleaded the cause of his country, addressing the four
deferential and reserved figures on the tribunal, in English. Tremendous curiosity was excited by the appearance of this one King in the midst of diplomats and
statesmen. But Albert was too far above the crowd to
blend successfully with it, too outside it to play an effec-
tive part. Moreover, his rôle was distasteful to him.
He hated to act as his own ambassador; and on the rare
occasions when his Ministers persuaded him to intervene in person, he insisted that the gist of the matter
should be written down, whether it were to be discussed
with Lord Curzon or whether it were to be voiced on
behalf of Belgium in the debates at Versailles.

Lloyd George was incapable of understanding him.
A number of years later, in 1931, the King said to me:
"In my opinion, Lloyd George's ruling passion is spite.

He was actuated by spite, for instance, in the way he mangled the Hapsburg Empire. . . ." I do not know whether David Lloyd George had made tactless remarks in his presence. Clémenceau most certainly had, yet the King had an unconcealed admiration for the Tiger, who returned it in full. His visit to La Panne in 1918 had been most affecting, and a spice had been added to it by the fact that the enemy artillery had sighted the cars in which the King and Clémenceau were driving, and had done them the honour to bombard them right royally. The two great leaders had been forced to alter their itinerary. The King and Clémenceau had at least one thing in common—their indifference to danger— and the memory of this War episode delighted them both. But once the heroic hour was over, they had few thoughts that took the same road. When Albert met Clémenceau at Versailles, he hinted to him that his mania for dethroning all the Princes of Central Europe might constitute a serious menace to the Peace.

"Oh, Kings . . . hardly two of them in a century are worth a thought," the Tiger retorted casually. Perhaps he was under the impression that he was voicing an indirect compliment, but the King turned a deaf ear to "compliments" of this kind. Thus, when Foch said to him: "I was obliged to go to Italy in 1917, and rescue poor King Victor Emmanuel by the skin of his teeth," the King considered the jest in execrable taste and never forgot it. Yet it was not that he envied the glory of others; I am sure that no such thought ever crossed his mind. He always showed a boundless admiration for great men, but this spontaneous respect

did not admit of familiarity. Now Foch was familiar, a *bon enfant* brought up in a Republic where Kings were curiosities, not powers. The King always preferred Joffre, because he was simpler, more primitive, and accepted with Olympian calm all the decrees of Fate. The victor of the Marne always struck him as being a man of action, and the King hated unnecessary speech. "I have a great esteem for Marshal Pétain because he never speaks unless he has something to say," he told M. Janson. "I visited the front with him. He used to talk to the officers, and invariably found something fresh to tell them without wasting words." It was Marshal Pétain whom he requested to find an officer to act as tutor to his son, the future Leopold III; and Major Plée, chosen for this high mission, was a witness of the friendship between the two great soldiers for many years.

It was useless to expect the King to remain on intimate terms with famous men. He knew that his name was written with theirs in the Annals of the Great, and this sufficed him. He disliked Lloyd George and respected Clémenceau, but he never spent a day of leisure with either. Philosophically, he held himself serenely aloof from current events. He had sloughed all his bitter feelings against Germany and the Germans. Dead-set against the financial terms of the Treaty of Versailles, a sceptical supporter of the Occupation of the Ruhr, he considered that his place in history entitled him to talk freely with the vanquished. He spoke of the Germans as a soldier would speak, without hatred or fear.

Edward VII always took his Ministers or confidential advisers with him on his travels; Albert I travelled in order to escape from them. On some days it was almost like a game of hide-and-seek. I am not alluding to official travels, highly spectacular affairs, in the course of which he signed decrees stamped at Rio de Janeiro, Chicago or Calcutta. I refer to those times when the King would disappear for two or three days, no one knew where. When Leopold I deliberately indulged in similar escapades, his Ministers deplored them. When he wished to avoid signing a royal warrant, it had to be sent on to Nice, Lausanne or Hyères. These small subterfuges were in keeping with his nature. But Albert I never resorted to ruses of ·this kind, which were repugnant to his innate integrity. His were the tricks of a schoolboy trying to evade an imposition; he would appear at a boring reception for exactly the necessary length of time—from two o'clock till four o'clock—and would then vanish, as he had come, no one knew whence or whither.

Three days later the Ministers would learn from a brief notice in the papers that the King would return on the following day after *a very short sojourn* in Switzerland. Filled with amazement, they would prepare to welcome a ruler refreshed and restored after his holiday. On his return, he would talk serenely of current affairs, as if for those three days he had remained bound to the remorselessly-growing pile of documents submitted for his signature. We can imagine what a task it must have been to go through the heap of official papers that had accumulated in his brief absence. A

Minister's arm ached at the end of a day spent in countersigning documents that began with the sacred formula: "We, Albert"; and the King's fingers must have been completely nerveless by the time he had put his signature to all the papers he had left untouched during those days of recreation.

His holidays were the only matters on which he would take no one's advice. His Kingship had absorbed him entirely—but his leisure hours were his own. He would submit to impositions and deprivations of every kind, but he would never give up his car, his aeroplane or his mountaineering—all that satisfied his love of danger. On one occasion only, M. Delacroix ventured a respectful protest in the name of the Ministry against the flying exploits of their Sovereign. Little did it avail. He received a polite and brief reply in which the underlying irony was only too apparent.

But when we pass from intellect to feeling, we no longer find an immovable rock but a sensitive human being. He would often say that Baudouin, his elder brother, had been exceptionally high-strung. In 1890 that tall, excitable youth, whose moods had changed at a mere shadow or an abruptly spoken word, must have reminded many people of certain characters in Paul Bourget's books. He was a keen officer and had an attractive personality, yet he suffered acutely from melancholia. "Had my brother become King, this excess of emotion would have made him very unhappy," the King would say. It was known in Brussels that he himself was liable to sudden fits of rage, that he nursed bitter grudges, and experienced alternate moods of de-

pression and exaltation. He swung from one extreme to the other so frequently that politicians said of him: "The King always agrees with the last speaker." This was not quite true, but the last speaker did invariably produce an effect, unconscious though it might be. If he were an optimist, the King would listen to him reluctantly. If he were a pessimist, he heard him with equal disfavour; but when the audience was over, he would pursue for hours, perhaps for days, the black butterflies of his dark imaginings.

What subtle part did reading play in this strange psychology? What effect did newspapers have on the King? How much did books influence him, from scientific works down to those stories of adventure in which he found an antidote, a new means of escape? His table was heaped with novels by Pierre Benoît, Claude Farrère, and other writers; there was even Céline's enormously long *Voyage au Bout de la Nuit,* which he had read right through from cover to cover. He always insisted on cutting the pages himself, because it gave his hands something to do. He remembered every word in the *Mercure de France;* and to the amazement of his secretaries, he treasured every copy of this review, to which he had subscribed for twenty years. As early as nine o'clock in the morning a mound of printed matter began to accumulate by his desk. He had long acquired the expert's eye which can pick out the most important article in each paper, its essential meaning, the exact significance of every heading. Since he took everything seriously, even the most hastily written article was of interest to him.

He took far too much notice of what journalists said. After he had scrutinized the *Quotidien, L'Œuvre,* and *L'Action Française,* and had perused the lengthy columns of the *Times* and the *Berliner Tageblatt,* he turned to the Belgian press. How avidly he read the national newspapers, always ready to scent some cause for offence. A trifle was enough to wound and depress him, a mere piece of thoughtlessness would bring back the hopeless refrain of his reign to his lips: "My people do not like me. . . ." Let me add that the journalists of a capital like Brussels are a race of bohemians, an excitable and sceptical crew, who will drip honey from their pens between two vitriolic attacks. This the King could not know. Nor could he know that behind an explosive article there often lurked an amused observer ironically judging the effect of his bombshell. If one were to listen daily to the chorus of the Belgian press, unaware of what was going on behind the scenes, one would indubitably conclude that the Belgians hate the Belgians.

The King drank deep draughts of this poison-brew of discord. In his extraordinary study at Laeken, with the map of the world, the endless files, and the canary, he dissected these articles line by line with a morbid intensity. Did he ever think at such moments of the delirious welcome the Chamber had given him on August 4, 1914, when he had uttered the celebrated words: "When I look round on this profoundly moved assembly which has only one thought . . ."? Friends sometimes tried to make him speak of that stirring time; but he would shake his head, as if embarrassed by

his own greatness, and would bury himself in his news-papers, muttering: "Obviously, so-and-so thinks I am no good—no good at all. Have you read his article?"

He himself rarely rebuked an erring journalist. But there were some matters in which he could brook no criticism, the chief of which was the honour of his fam-ily. In this respect he had very little of the Parisian in him, but was sensitive to a degree. Did he think of the curses heaped on the memory of Leopold II? Until the death of the old King, Albert had lived in the virtuous atmosphere of the Palace of Flanders, where any allu-sion to the escapades of his uncle was made with low-ered eyes. He certainly flared up at the slightest refer-ence to any imaginary indiscretion attributed to a mem-ber of his family. I remember an article about the Emperor Maximilian of Mexico. A book had been pub-lished on his life, making him out to be regrettably com-plaisant; and the article had echoed this accusation in all good faith. The King flew into a violent rage, and the Premier was compelled to read the unfortunate author a severe lecture. Incidentally, the King subse-quently showed him much kindness. It may be asked whether Albert were not wasting his time in giving the lie to statements that the public so quickly forgot. The public has a very short memory. The King's was fiend-ishly retentive; he never knew that restful state which we call indifference; and apart from those times when he was striding amongst the mountains or was finding escape from the world in the enchanted realm of books, his thoughts must have been a perpetual torment.

Even the greatest men, as they age, are apt to babble,

and the King had a horror of growing garrulous. The incense of adulation may turn the heads of even the most hardened statesmen, but the King only breathed it in with irritation, as if it were too prodigally diffused. He had had too much of the heady draught of popularity; he never desired it, and was convinced that he would die poor and forgotten. He who had so little money sense, had given up spending, travelled third-class, had no wants, and deplored the fact that his reign was "a twopenny-halfpenny affair." In this same reign, Albert evoked the glory of Leopold II, and expended his energy in defending his memory at a time when no one was thinking of attacking it. He would request that the publication date of various articles should be hastened, and when editors did not immediately comply he grew angry and suspicious. Hundreds of thousands of men would gladly have died for him without a moment's hesitation; he must have sensed this; but of two points of view he invariably chose the gloomier. Those who advised him in his hours of happiness assuredly never dreamed that their words would recur to him so bitterly in his hours of darkness, never dreamed that the King, the soul of honour, always lent a willing ear to gossip-mongers.

The truth is, that he never appreciated the glorious adventure of his life. Again and again he would mutter between his teeth: "My people do not love me."

One Sunday he started off by car for the fêtes which were being held in a certain town. As they drove along, the King began to confide in his aide-de-camp, and the dialogue began: "The people of X . . . do not like me.

In my heart of hearts, I don't know why I'm going. On a Sunday, too. There won't be a soul there. They'll all be out in the country. The only people who will be there are the officials who hope to get a decoration."

The King arrived. The bells pealed. The roads were thronged, the balconies were thronged, the very roofs were thronged. The crowd of officials performed their duties adequately, and everything went swimmingly. The King saluted, his face impassive, almost indifferent, and left, after having voiced his thanks and congratulations to all. On the way back, the conversation was resumed.

"Happily, Your Majesty was mistaken. There was a huge crowd."

To which the King, buried in a corner of the car, replied, in a semi-serious tone: "Yes, there will be a similar crowd when I am led to the scaffold."

How often on his return from some dull ceremonial he would sigh: "One did not put up much of a show. . . ." *One* meant himself, that strange being who was always infuriated by his imaginary shortcomings. Such moods might be caused by a trifle—perhaps by a long-drawn-out speech in which the orator had repeated over and over again that the King had saved the army on the Yser, and that he would be known to history as the Warrior King.

At such moments a mere trifle was enough to depress or delight him. In 1930, in the midst of the Centenary Celebrations, he remarked philosophically: "I am rather like that Sultan who had so many wives that no fresh bride could give him any pleasure. I have re-

ceived many ovations, but I have read enough history to realize that they are ephemeral. Louis XVI was acclaimed, so was Nicholas II. And so were the Hapsburgs. . . . I may be applauded a little more or a little less. . . . This applause will neither hasten nor delay the decrees of Fate. . . . I am accused of being a Socialist. I am disliked in conservative circles. But, like the Sultan, I am used to it. Leopold II was as well aware of all this as I am. When I was a young man, I remember accompanying him to assemblies of Brussels doctrinaires, who gave us a very cold reception. Don't you remember them? No, you were too young. There will be more of them in the future. . . ."

Seated opposite him in an arm-chair exactly like his own, I eagerly scanned the play of his features. His gaze was abstracted, there was a faint expression of irony on his face—he was playing the part of master-sceptic. A *tête-à-tête* with him would sometimes last a long while and turn into amazing channels. On this occasion he began to speak of Leopold II.

"The people are utterly hypocritical. They have execrated the memory of Leopold II because of his *liaison* with Madame Vaughan. But the excuses for his conduct have been deliberately overlooked. He was married against his will to a foreign Princess who was practically a stranger to him, and he did neither more nor less than the sons of our great industrialists. He had made a marriage of convenience, which brought him nothing but misery. Late in life, he fell in love with another woman whom, moreover, he married. A mountain was made of this molehill. I have often dis-

cussed it with Cardinal Mercier, who agreed with me that we ought to make allowances for this great and unhappy man. . . . But there are some people who refuse to understand. . . ."

He spoke with an air of resentment. He obviously wanted me to repeat his words. At the time I was far from believing that the occasion would, alas, so soon arise when I should quote them. But I could clearly imagine the conversation between the King and the Cardinal, two men equally good and equally great, both stern critics of themselves, both indulgent towards the failings of others, both anxious to excuse flagrant peccadilloes which people in Belgium had long ceased to discuss. But for their spiritual grandeur, it might have been said that they were wasting their time. On those heights where they lived and breathed, they forgot that the young Belgians of 1931 did not even know who Madame Vaughan was, and that the old had exhausted the subject.

The duologue between the public who looked at the King without seeing him, and the King who saw the public without appearing to look at it, might have endured for another twenty years. The majority of the people never dreamed that the King knew them so well. They merely said that he must belong to a special order of human beings, and in this they were perfectly right. He resembled none of his subjects, but the nature of this difference escaped them all. Journalists attempted to define it in their articles, unaware that the King noted the mistakes they made, with an ominous look on his face.

As for his Ministers, although he treated them, as has been said, with affability and patience, they had a vague suspicion that a wide gap separated them from their Sovereign. The fact that the King so often disappeared and played truant like a schoolboy sometimes caused the Premier surprise; he would not have been so surprised, however, had he had access to the collection of Alpine reviews and pamphlets on mountaineering that were heaped on Albert's table. The King loved Switzerland, the tiny aerial world where he was at last left in peace amidst the glaciers and meadows that sparkled with pristine dew. Tactless holiday-makers followed him persistently at St. Moritz. He turned on them like a lion at bay, snatched their cameras and dashed them to the ground. They wanted to steal his mountain. He never went to St. Moritz again. In his study at Brussels, hung with buttercup-yellow silk, there was a landscape done in crude greens. It was a picture of Lake Kivu, in that beloved country where the vast tracts that bear his name had been set apart at his command for the preservation of volcanic flora and fauna. He would often gaze affectionately at this canvas which evoked the land of sun and sleep. The picture was hanging there a few days before his death. I believe it is hanging there still.

Only those who saw the King on ceremonial occasions and subsequently heard his sympathetic or ironic comments, could form any idea of the anomaly of the part he played. The people, even the inhabitants of Brussels, did not realize the depth of his discernment.

I remember a distinguished historian, who had seen the King at some ceremony, saying to me: "I watched him closely. He kept perfectly motionless the whole time, and evidently never saw a thing. Anyhow, he is very near-sighted. But how admirably he does what is expected of him." Which only goes to prove that even a historian can be mistaken. Certainly, nothing could be more difficult than to gauge the feelings of a King on official occasions. At least it may be said of Albert that he was neither unhearing nor unseeing, and that while he only turned a blank mask to the public, he hid mercilessly acute impressions behind his glasses.

On Saints' Days he would drive in his state coach, in accordance with tradition, to St. Gudule. Here, in the tragic and solemn Cathedral, the memories of the history of Belgium formed a triumphal procession for him. Here, on the crimson dais, in the enchantment created by the marble effigies, the magnificent pulpit carved by Verbruggen and the dreamlike windows painted by Rozier, the huge stature of the King made him look like a knight of old. Here were buried the Dukes of Burgundy, those Dukes who dazzled the greatest Courts of Europe with their splendour; here the Golden Fleece held its two Chapters, and here Philip II of Spain caused a Mass to be read for Charles V, Emperor of the West. Here, before the mausoleum had been built at Laeken, reposed the bodies of Leopold I the Mentor of Europe, Leopold II the Navigator, and Desiré Joseph, Cardinal Mercier. Here the muffled drums were beaten when the troops set out for the front in 1914; here, too, they sounded again for the triumphal

return in 1918; for the marriage of Leopold-Philippe-Charles-Albert-Meinrad-Hubert-Marie-Miguel, Duke of Brabant, Prince of Belgium, Duke of Saxe, Prince of Saxe-Coburg-Gotha, to Princess Astrid of Sweden, when they passed beneath the crossed swords of the Guard. Here, at the shrine of St. Albert, the people of Brussels proclaimed their loyalty and faith during the four years of the War, as if even then it was their desire to canonize their beloved leader. A red carpet ran like a flame to the altar. The King appeared, his eyes dimmed by his glasses, those eyes that saw and retained everything. In the austere majesty of the Cathedral the *Domine, salvum fac regem* arose, and the King for whom the blessings of Heaven were being so fervently invoked—the King had already noted who was absent, and had taken in every detail of the ceremony.

When he visited the devastated areas with M. van de Vyvère, in 1920, he caught sight of a notice on which some malcontents had underlined the figures of the Civil List.

At Malines, in 1930, he observed two seditious seminarists who were leaning against a wall and refused to salute. As he passed through Louvain, a few fanatics shrieked insults at him. He went on his way, magnificently indifferent, betraying no sign that he had heard. That night, he remarked casually: "Did you notice how ugly, spotty, and unshaven those young men were?"

Yet at heart he feared these Belgians whom he loved so much, and over whom he watched like a guardian angel. I have often thought that the world appeared

to Albert I in the shape of a multitude of malevolent
demons, whose faces were familiar, and that every
morning a mocking spirit whispered in his ear: "Be-
ware! . . ."

The King wore out many of his friends. No one ever
knew exactly why he could be so warm at one moment,
so cold the next.

Naturally, M. Vandervelde was the most favoured,
because he was Republican yet Royalist, a patriot yet
an internationalist, an irreproachable Minister yet a
revolutionary, a fire-brand in his speeches yet entirely
the reverse in his hierarchic relations. Above all, when
he was in office he had the rare tact to consult the King
at every moment; and Albert, while he never ceded a
point, was none the less subtly flattered. To sum up, M.
Vandervelde had as great an admiration for the King's
mental powers as for his character and, as he never showered cheap adulation on him, he put him at his ease.
The King fulminated against M. Vandervelde and said:
"He is more than an adversary, he is a rival. . . ." But
he esteemed him as a great man, and knew that his
esteem was returned in full. Their gratitude and appreciation was mutual, but neither would give way to
the other. When M. Anseele, a true Socialist, was
shown many little attentions by the Queen, M. Ruzette
remarked to M. Vandervelde: "It strikes me that Anseele is lapping it up." To which M. Vandervelde replied: "Yes, Anseele has remained a child of the people." But at heart he himself was just as gratified by
such attentions. He was, however, more intellectual

than emotional. Provided that his mind had full scope, he had no further desires. Yet he had the same failings of temper as his fellow men. One day he flew into a furious passion in the King's presence, and Albert was incensed. It was not enough, therefore, to be President of the second Internationale to remain in His Majesty's good graces.

Friendships swept through the Palace of Brussels *sicut foenum agri,* like chaff on the wind. Some were restored, others departed for ever; it needed death, illness or a great personal sorrow to touch the King's innate kindness, cause him to come impulsively forth from his splendid isolation, and lavish treasures of sympathy and pity.

So the years after the War passed away, the years when the King, burdened by his world-wide renown, was bound by the chains of small constitutional tasks. One morning he was present at the great manœuvres at Beverloo. I had been allowed to wear uniform again and ride in his suite. When we reached the top of the knoll he made me take the place beside him.

As usual he was riding Titanic, the huge Anglo-Norman horse which had been bought at Charolais from the stud of the Marquis de Croix. The King was in a good mood, and talked about the country of the Campine which lay before us. He reminded me of his early years: "In those days, the soldiers drilled in busbies, and were commanded by N.C.O.'s as tough as leather. It would be amusing to try and reckon up the oaths and imprecations that have accumulated for a century on this parade-ground. When I was a captain, I heard

every possible variation of bad language. . . ." He was delightful at such moments, with his acute sense of the ridiculous, his good taste in never airing his own knowledge, and in reminding you constantly of your own small attainments.

Down below, we could hear the put-put-put of machine-guns, the sound of bugles, and the rumble of tanks that were advancing like prehistoric monsters. Presently he began to talk of his Ministers. He was genuinely attached to M. Jaspar and M. Theunis, but he felt sure that some of the others disregarded him. "You might make a charming book one day by collecting all the advice given by Leopold I, Leopold II and myself, and which has never been taken," he said to me. "We have all three of us been answered by bowings and scrapings and promises, and that's the end of it. They take us for fools. . . ." I was surprised that he should express himself so freely to a novice. Perhaps he was revenging himself in some small way on the exalted by telling the lowly—in this case, myself—why he preferred to keep his own counsel. Later on he lectured me, too, and gave me a dressing-down, but that morning at Beverloo he was absolutely natural. He was in the midst of his soldiers, far from his study in Brussels, temporarily care-free; and as he talked, Titanic pawed the soil of Belgium where, despite their shortcomings, seven million human beings loved and served him so well.

It is very difficult to know who his real friends were. Included amongst them, there was certainly M. Lippens, the Governor-General of the Congo, and the Presi-

dent of the Senate. M. Ingenbleek was undoubtedly listened to and loved. After 1916, the King used to say: "I have lost a friend . . . my best friend." This was M. Waxweiler, the Socialist. He was killed in a motor accident in London.

General de Grunne died in 1926, General Jungbluth in 1930. The former, a widower in the evening of his life, had divided his property amongst his children, handed his sword to the King, retired to the Benedictine Abbey of Maredsous, and had taken the vows. With scrupulous conscientiousness and the joy which springs from sacrifice freely accepted, he had performed all the rites of the novitiate laid down by the rule of the Blessed Father. The first impression the new monk had made on the novice-master was that he was the victim of an illusion and had no real vocation, but after a few days he changed his mind. The General advanced step by step along the Narrow Path with a discipline that was entirely military, setting a good example to the young Brothers by his sweet temper and devout piety; he only left his new abode in order to christen his great-grandchildren. When he took his final vows in the presence of his children, grandchildren and great-grandchildren, the King wrote a most beautiful letter to his old master, in which he spoke of the joy of giving oneself to God.

In his old age the General, who had become almost completely blind, said the same Mass all the year round, and his prayers were limited to meditation and the Rosary. His greatest enjoyment still lay in describing the battles of the Empire, and in narrating once more

for the interest of his brother monks the battles of Marengo, Champaubert, Montmirail, Rezonville and Sedan. He had a profound admiration for the victory of Tannenberg; he would spread out the map which he could no longer see, and point out places whose positions he knew by heart. "On the left there, you see the Mazura Lakes," he would say. "That's where Hindenburg discovered the weakness—a classic manœuvre." To distract him, the monks would read passages from the *History of the Second Empire* by La Gorce, and he would interrupt with comments and anecdotes about his father-in-law and his family. His gaiety was unfailing. When the monastery bell rang for the midday meal, he would come out of his cell, make an imaginary bugle with his hand, and blow the Belgian equivalent for "Come and get it." It had taken the General a journey of forty years to go from the Abbey of La Cambre to that of Maredsous; but he now obeyed the Benedictine rules as easily as he had kept the military regulations.

Jungbluth, though, never knew the fragrance of the fir-trees of Maredsous, never heard the song of the Molinié which flows at the foot of its hill. He died in Brussels whilst the King and General Swaeger were making their flight to Bagdad. Jungbluth, who had never married, died quite alone, leaving behind him very few acquaintances and not one intimate friend. The army had been his only passion, and his profession had moulded him to such an extent that at eighty years of age his figure remained as elegant, stiff and upright as ever, In military circles the story ran that he rested

his foot on the sill when he laced his shoes, in order to preserve his suppleness. It was also said that he was a Jew and a Freemason, but this was never confirmed—everything about him was wrapped in mystery. Up till 1914, he had kept a diary of his thoughts, but he had left it behind in his house in Brussels; and a servant, thinking that it might contain facts that had better not be exposed to the curiosity of the Germans, had burnt it before a visit of inspection could take place. Thus, once again, documents relating to the Court of Brussels vanished.

During the course of his career, Jungbluth had reached the zenith of success and sunk to the nadir of disfavour and disgrace. He belonged to the traditional type of the Great Ones of the earth, for he had governed a King with absolute dominion, and had later been flung aside during a change of mood. He had left La Panne, and had gone to spend three of the War years at Le Havre in the so-called Royal Villa where the King and Queen never went. Since then he had been reinstated, but the aides-de-camp were sometimes surprised at the haughty way in which the King spoke to him. The memorial service for Jungbluth was not held in St. Gudule till the King's return from the East. Albert was deeply moved; and an odd fancy struck me when I saw the procession leaving the Cathedral. The crowd of dignitaries and officers bowed as the King passed them, and it seemed as though they were trying to visualize at his side the gaunt silhouette and austere expression of the man who had followed his royal master at all ceremonies of this kind for forty long years.

CHAPTER XIII

THE KING IS DEAD

THE last year of the King's life seems to have been the happiest. Success had crowned his efforts in every sphere. In 1926, the Duke of Brabant married the Princess of his choice. On September 27 of that year the King had summoned the representatives of the Brussels press. He looked unusually happy and said: "I have asked you to come here, gentlemen, in order to announce the engagement of my eldest son." He then enumerated the titles of the bride-to-be, a Swedish Princess, the third daughter of Prince Charles, the King of Sweden's brother, and of Princess Ingeborg, sister of the King of Denmark. "My son met Princess Astrid while he was travelling in Scandinavia," added the King. "He met her again at the christening of Prince Michael, the infant son of Prince Réné of Bourbon." His voice shook slightly as he ended: "They found that they loved each other, and have decided to get married. Their parents cannot but rejoice at this engagement between two young people who are so deeply in love."

That was all. When the King spoke thus, there was nothing to be added. Thenceforth, the love story of his son belonged to the Belgian people; and as soon as Princess Astrid set foot on the quay at Antwerp, they showed that they had understood. The bells pealed, and the papers were full of names and photographs of

of Nordic Princes, for all the Scandinavian Royalties
are related to one another. A great number of them
were present at the wedding. They were tall and slim,
with the physique of skiing champions, and were as
much at home in a Socialist country as at the tennis
parties given by the officers on their staffs.

The new Duchess of Brabant was extremely pretty—
a most important consideration in the eyes of the Belgian people. And her popularity was assured when
Belgium realized that she lived only for her husband,
and was interested in all his affairs down to the smallest
detail. She accompanied him on his long travels to
India and the Congo, was tireless and tactful, would
rush from liner to aeroplane, and was as ready to visit
a hospital in the Tropics as a crèche in Brussels. Princess Astrid had come to an enlightened Court, where
the children, like their parents, had a taste for solid
reading and scientific study.

Her husband had inherited a large share of his
father's mental gifts—those gifts which had been so ignored in Albert during his youth. He had only had
mediocre tutors, but he had seen to it that his son had
the best in Belgium, as well as the finest library and
every opportunity for travel. At twenty Prince Leopold had been taught history by Professor Pirenne, the
science of war by Colonel Plée, Flemish literature by
Teirlinck, the dramatist, the principles of religion by
Cardinal Mercier, and geography by world travel. In
addition to the knowledge he had acquired, he had cul-
tivated the family passion for natural history, miner-
alogy and agriculture. He was particularly interested

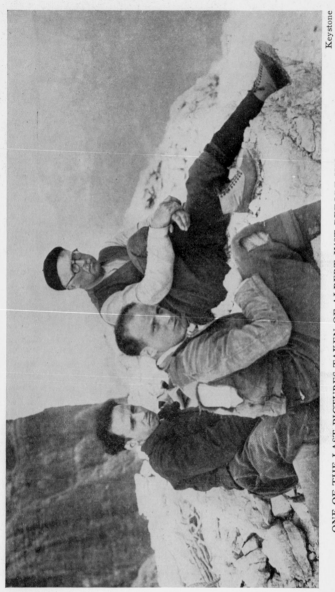

ONE OF THE LAST PICTURES TAKEN OF ALBERT JUST BEFORE HIS TRAGIC DEATH

in the flora and fauna of the tropics. He had been twice to India, and once to the Congo, accompanied by professors, the Director of the Natural History Museum, and the Minister of Colonial Agriculture.

Princess Astrid had become a Catholic. "I am glad, very glad," the King had repeated on the day she was received into the Faith. "Now all the family is united in the same religion." The church bells had pealed forth for a christening, for two christenings. On each occasion the beautiful golden coaches had set out, escorted by squadrons of Guides, to the joyful sound of bugles and carillons.

Princess Marie-José was living abroad and was not so well known in Belgium as her brothers. The people of Brussels, less easily overawed by grandeur than the English in such matters, had been only moderately impressed by her marriage to a future King. Prince Umberto was blessed with good looks and a charming personality; but directly after the wedding he had taken his bride to Italy, where she had been entirely absorbed into the Italian Royal Family. Instead of a gift received, it was a gift bestowed. The fact that Princess Marie-José lived so far from her own country gave rise to rumours that she was not happy. They were entirely unfounded; but circumstances had prevented Prince Umberto from visiting Brussels after his marriage, and this lent weight to the gossip.

The King saw his daughter most frequently in Switzerland. "She is a great comfort to me," he wrote. With the pride which many fathers feel in their young-

est-born, he thought she was the most brilliant of all
his children, the most "Leopoldian"; and he would repeat: "She ought to have been the heir to the throne."

By the beginning of 1934, the King was able to assure
himself that there was no monarchic question in Belgium—or rather, that the question had not arisen. Although, in principle, the Ministers acted independently
of the King, his opinion was taken more and more into
account. A Minister might hold different views—he was
entitled to do so—but with the passing of the years the
King's prerogative had come to exceed that of the Ministers. Moreover, it would have been most unwise for
a Minister to call down the Royal displeasure on his
head. The King's prerogative was a privilege of very
long standing. None of this was formulated, nor was
it exacted, least of all by the King.

The Sovereign was at last appearing as the supreme
guardian of the Constitution. Trouble arose between
the Government and ex-servicemen; hundreds of them
disregarded the police regulations and swarmed into the
neutral zone surrounding the Ministries. There was
only one man who could make these angry men see
reason. The King spoke to them, and his words made
so great an impression on them that their menacing attitude changed to one of quiet respect. Thus there
was one in Belgium who towered above the Government. He had only to raise his little finger to calm a
crowd that would have shouted down both the Ministers
and its own leaders.

On that Saturday, February 17, 1934, the King rose at
the same early hour as usual, read his mail, glanced
through the daily mound of newspapers, and gave several audiences. He had promised to preside that evening at a meeting of cyclists at the Palace of Sport,
where Scherens, the young Flemish World-Champion,
was to appear. Cycling is a very popular sport in Belgium, where the people do not care for gambling but
adore speed contests. The King liked to display an
interest in all the healthy diversions of his subjects.
At twelve-fifteen, wearied by his morning's work, and
with the prospect of an official ceremony looming before
him, he was seized by a longing for fresh air and exercise.

"I am going climbing near Namur," he told the
Queen. "I shall be away some hours. . . ."

Owing to the time of year, it was impossible to do
any climbing after five o'clock. The car was brought
round. His only escort was Van Dyck, his valet; the
King himself took the wheel, and they rapidly reached
the road to Namur. No one noticed the driver with his
cap and large round glasses. The car skirted the capital.
The Namur road is an excellent and much-used thoroughfare. On the sixty-mile run the King passed
through one of the richest regions of his kingdom—
Flemish Brabant and Walloon Brabant. At Overrijsche
he passed the statue of Justus Lipsus, the famous phi-
losopher of the Renaissance. The country grew increasingly hilly.

Namur was the last stage of his journey, and he had
only to follow the Meuse to the village of Marche-les-

Dames. Here a wall of rock overhangs the river. This is old feudal Wallonia, where the Abbey of Marche-les-Dames held sway for centuries, subsequently bequeathing its lands to the Dukes of Arenberg. The Grotto at Marche-les-Dames is well known to students of archaeology on account of its prehistoric remains. At the foot of the cliff there is a path and a garishly painted Calvary, called by the peasants the Gentle God of Pity. On the opposite bank stands the château of Brumages, gleaming white under a slate roof.

Here the King drew up. It was a romantic scene, full of historic association and local tradition, a symphony in black and silver—grey rocks, gleaming river and stark trees, whose skeleton boughs were outlined against the sky. It was barely three o'clock. I will let those who were there that day describe what happened. Far too many false rumours have already arisen about that fatal night; and it is better to keep to bare statements.

The following particulars were collected by Dumont-Wilden. I myself checked them minutely on the actual spot, and made notes. His description is accurate in every detail.

"When the King reached the rocks he intended to climb, he walked about alone for some time to take his bearings, decided to ascend to the plateau that commands a view of the cliff, and go through the woods in the direction of the car which he had left near the small village of Boninne. Shortly before he had reached the plateau the King stopped and said to Van Dyck:

" 'Follow the path for another fifty yards. I shall

take advantage of the remaining daylight to go down to the foot of the rocks and make an ascent from there. I will join you at about four o'clock or four-thirty.'

"As Van Dyck knew his master well, and understood his need to be alone, he was in no way surprised, and waited as he had been told.

"An hour passed, an hour and a quarter, an hour and a half. Van Dyck was puzzled, because he knew that the King intended to be at the Palace of Sport at the time that had been fixed; from being puzzled, he grew uneasy, and decided to set out in search of his master. It was growing dark. The ground over which the King had ventured was difficult: a thicket overgrown with brambles and strewn with boulders. Van Dyck felt his way along, calling in increasingly anxious tones. There was no answer—the country was wrapped in the silence of night. Suddenly, the King's faithful servant, who did not know what to think and was beginning to grow terrified, found himself confronted by a sheer wall of rock. He decided to retrace his steps to the main road, telephone for help, and warn the Palace of Laeken. He dashed into the village of Marche-les-Dames, where he managed to get into communication with the Palace. It was now seven o'clock. The King's absence had begun to cause surprise; Van Dyck's message gave rise to uneasiness, though all tried to convince themselves that it was only some trifling mishap which had delayed the King. Perhaps he had lost his way or sprained his ankle. . . . In any case, the Queen must be spared any unnecessary anxiety. Captain Jacques de Dixmude, the King's orderly, jumped into his car and drove rap-

idly to Marche-les-Dames. From there he was to telephone as soon as he had any news. Those at the Palace
waited in vain for him to ring up. A telephone message was then sent to Count Xavier de Grunne."

Count de Grunne's story is as follows:—

"At eight o'clock, I was informed of the King's in-
explicable absence, and immediately suggested that Dr.
Nolf, his physician and also his friend and companion,
should be fetched. There was some difficulty in finding
him, so that we were not able to start until eight-thirty.
At nine-forty-five we arrived on the scene, where Captain Jacques and two gendarmes were searching every
inch of the road beneath the cliff. Captain Jacques,
however, knew nothing about the configuration of the
district or the habits of climbers, and had no idea how
to proceed with the search. Van Dyck had just left
with the chauffeur for Boninne; could he have made a
mistake, had the King gone straight back to the car?
The presence of Van Dyck was essential for the carrying on of the search, and we awaited him anxiously,
examining the country round the needle that was said
to be 'inaccessible,' in our desire to be doing something.

"Ten-thirty. His Majesty's valet returned at last, and
helped, to some extent, to narrow down the field of our
search by telling us what he knew. I instantly decided
to begin systematically exploring the rock wall as far
as the Calvary. Unfortunately, this was very difficult
ground. The King had often climbed this part of the
cliff with me. While Jacques, Dr. Nolf and Baron Carton de Wiart (who had arrived in the meantime) were
examining the lower ledges and all accessible spots by

the feeble light of lanterns, I began the ascent by the usual path. If the King had met with an accident, his body might have lodged in one of the crevasses which mountaineers call chimneys, and which they make use of to help them in their ascents. There happens to be a chimney six feet wide and eighteen feet high in the cliff which overhangs the Meuse; this is known as the Louise Chimney. On several occasions the King had followed it with myself and others. I now climbed it again, flashing my electric torch into corners and crevices. This took me a long time, for I needed both hands to get to the top, and I found nothing. I came down on the other side along a slope covered with leaves, keeping close to the rock wall so that I could examine the ground carefully within a radius of about fifteen yards. At the moment, I did not dream that a body which had fallen from the summit could have rolled further than this. Here I was wrong, as will be seen later. In the meantime, I rejoined my companions, whose search had been as fruitless as my own. It was now eleven-fifteen. We began a similar operation on the left face of the cliff, but this, too, proved useless. By twelve-fifteen our anxiety was agonizing. We had to try every means in our power, and we now decided to send for five expert climbers, who were thoroughly acquainted with these rocks. While the chauffeur was on his way to Namur to ring them up, we carried on the search, but this time in a different part of the rocks, a part that was more frequently climbed. We met with no success. One-thirty A.M. While we waited for the climbers, for whom a car had been sent, Dr. Nolf, Baron

Carton de Wiart and Captain Jacques combed the undergrowth, even at some distance from the cliff; it was possible that the wounded man had dragged himself along for some distance, and had then lost consciousness. We were helped by the gendarmes and two foresters."

And now Count de Grunne tells the story of the terrible discovery:

"At one-fifty-five A.M., I came back to the road, suddenly overwhelmed by despair; the ascents in the dark which had lasted nearly four hours, during which my anxiety had been steadily growing, had completely exhausted me. At this moment, Captain Jacques, who, too, was beginning to feel hopeless, was hailed by Baron Carton de Wiart, and began to descend the leafy slope behind the Rock of the Gentle God, which I myself had followed after exploring the Louise Chimney at about eleven-fifteen. Suddenly he uttered a cry of horror. He had caught his foot in a rope, and had seen that this rope was attached to a body."

This is the story of the witnesses. I have since questioned all of them, and have made the same objection that several others have raised: that it would have been wiser to have warned police headquarters at Namur from the very beginning, as bloodhounds would have been put at their disposal. In reply, I was told that their first care that night had been to search all possible paths a climber might have taken, and that the experts they had sent for, the usual companions of the King's ascents, were better qualified to be of use than the police. Whether they were right or wrong, here is the

report of the Namur police after the body was brought back in the early hours of the morning:

"His Majesty, having begun the ascent of a rocky peak, reached the top, where traces of his footprints can plainly be seen. It would seem as though the King leant against a boulder which, on account of its size, he must have thought absolutely secure and firmly attached to the rock; this boulder evidently became dislodged, and dragged His Majesty down in its fall. The King struck a projecting ledge; traces of blood were found there this morning, and it must have been here that His Majesty received the wound which proved fatal. After his body had hit the ground, the impact caused it to rebound to a spot fifty yards lower down; various objects, a muffler, cap, knapsack and belt were scattered about in all directions, and were found by the police. The statements attached to this report were made on the spot by Count de Grunne and the official expert, and allow every stage of the tragic accident to be reconstructed exactly as it occurred."

Next, the search party, with the help of hastily summoned peasants, lifted the body of the King into a car. The secret had been so well kept that the villagers did not learn the identity of the dead man until the following morning. It was fitting that Belgian peasants, with their calloused and work-worn hands, should have been the first to raise their King—the King who had always loved them so dearly. High overhead, the crows were flapping their wings, seeking shelter in the hollow of the rocks. The broken body of the King was already

rigid in death—it was impossible to straighten it. It was laid on the floor of the car, "and the corpse, the arms still seeming as though they were trying to clutch at safety, kept toppling against the occupants of the car." It was a ghastly sight, covered with mud and blood. The cortège drove through Namur in silence, and reached Laeken before daybreak.

I have not made any alteration in this recital, as precise as a legal document. This was how the King died.

And it was just such a death as he would have chosen. He could not bear to be ill, and he was spared the humiliation of illness. He had a dread of growing old, and his last hours were spent in Herculean daring. He was the soul of bravery, and his last steps were the silent footfalls of a giant defying danger. He adored nature, loathed all ritual, and he died alone, at the foot of a Belgian cliff, facing the Meuse, in the light of day. All the members of the search party, even Dr. Nolf and Van Dyck, were his old comrades of the War years.

Only one human being had been able to distract him from his dark thoughts, his world-sickness; only one human being had been able to dissuade him from his escapes into the mountains. To her he had uttered his last farewell. Between that good-bye to the Queen at twelve-fifteen and his laconic remarks to Van Dyck, he had spoken no other word to any man. She alone had received his last thought, his last smile.

He might have come by this death in Switzerland, Austria or Italy . . . he died in Belgium. Belgium had earned this honour. So had he.

That Saturday night, all the spirits of darkness seemed
to have flocked to Brussels to do battle. At six o'clock,
I entered the Maison du Peuple, where the Socialists
had organized a great anti-Dolfuss meeting. The atmosphere of the hall was tense with excitement. The audience, whose feelings were at white heat, spoke of war,
the possibility of disaster, and the bombardment of the
workers' tenements in Vienna by the machine-guns of
the Chancellor-Dictator. The Red press in Brussels
had cunningly played upon the emotions of Belgian
workers by making them believe that the wind of Dic-
tatorship, blowing over Europe, was threatening Belgium and drawing near Brussels. The Internationalists
have always made use of these terrorist tactics. Sinister
figures crept into the hall. Excited groups were holding
discussions, and the street bore that ugly look which, to
the practised eye of the journalist, heralds the approach
of a strike.

If there were one word to describe that evening, that
word would be *"crisis."* There was crisis in the hearts
and minds of the people, crisis in affairs, crisis in ideals.
M. Brunfaut, a Brussels deputy, stood up on the platform. He was a tall, spectacled young man, with a fair
beard. Arms folded, he held forth ponderously; and
his repetition of the words "Friends . . . comrades
. . . our brothers in Vienna are dead . . ." achieved a
kind of pontifical success. He was like a Savonarola
uttering icy denunciations. He was followed by M.
Vandervelde, who was tired after a long series of conferences. As I came out, I saw two young Red guards
who had seized hold of a recalcitrant comrade. The

man swore vociferously, was jostled, lost his footing and fell into the gutter.

At about eleven o'clock a crowd of riff-raff, some two hundred in all, appeared near the Bourse and rushed along the boulevards, yelling: "Down with the skull-cap! Down with the priests! Down with the Church Dictators!" Two deputies, M. Spaak and M. Brunfaut, followed them reluctantly—they evidently felt things were going too far. The atmosphere was heavy with foreboding. The talk was entirely centred around the rioting in Paris and the bombardment in Vienna. The people in the boulevards looked on uneasily as the night-birds made for the offices of the *Nation Belge* in the Place de Brouckère. In a few minutes they had smashed every window. From the neighbouring alleys sinister figures surged forth as if by magic. The glass crashed to the ground with the brittle sound of hail-stones. Four or five revolver shots rang out in the night. The rioters made off, aware that the police were hastening to the scene in force, and battered down the gates of the College of St. Louis, while they continued to shout: "Down with Dolfuss! . . . Down with the skull-cap!" Men in dungarees and leather coats, half orators, half agitators, headed the crowd, still followed by the two reluctant Communist deputies—true symbols of demagogy dragged along by the chains of its own rhetoric.

It was cold and damp. At the Palais des Beaux Arts, Lord Robert Cecil was presiding at a Peace Conference, seated between M. Vandervelde and Père Rutten, the Dominican Father in his white robes. The huge hall

was filled, but there were more sceptics than believers among the audience. Arc lamps flung a crude light on the speakers, making them look ghastly pale. When I left, I again encountered the rioters, now surrounded by police. . . . No, the good angels invoked by Lord Robert Cecil and Father Rutten had given way that night to the powers of darkness. Men of good-will sought in vain for peace. St. Michael, the heavenly warrior who stands on the spire of the Hôtel de Ville, no longer trampled the gilded dragon underfoot—it was abroad, crawling sinuously through the shadowy streets; and the city, vaguely conscious of approaching disaster, was in the throes of an obscure unrest.

The newspaper offices passed an agitated night. Special editions had to be rushed out with reports of the Socialist riots. Towards three A.M. the rotary printing presses in the basement began their infernal cacophony. As the din started, I left the offices of the *Nation Belge,* never dreaming that at Laeken, at that very hour, the gravel was crunching softly beneath the wheels of two cars—so softly that the Queen, who slept on the first floor, never woke. Three hours later, after I had reached home, the telephone bell made me start. It was the news editor speaking. "The King is dead . . . come along at once."

Dawn was breaking. Rubbing my eyes, I arrived at the offices with their shattered windows. The disturbances of the night before seemed aeons distant. . . . The King was dead. The powers of darkness had vanished with the night, as though his soul, in passing, had

driven away the evil angels with the strong beat of its wings.

That evening I saw him once more in the room which had been his since 1909. The great chandelier cast a light on the pale green paper and the Empire bed. One of the servants of the household led me through the empty, brilliantly illuminated salons, and the gloomy study, where the canary was hopping mournfully in its cage. I saw his arm-chair, the map of the world, the Empire writing desk covered with photographs of his children and littered with papers. The salons wore an air of melancholy despite their festive array. The great crimson divans and chairs, now unoccupied, looked as though they were conferring mysteriously together. I passed through the deserted rooms, and came at last to his bedroom.

He lay in the centre of the bed, clad in the uniform of a Lieutenant-General, with the Grand Cordon of Leopold and the Croix de Guerre. His pale fingers held a tiny ivory crucifix, a gift from the workers of the Congo Mission—the delicately carved crucifix of which he had been fond. His head was swathed in wrappings, his right cheek was laid on the pillow. It was six o'clock. He had been embalmed at noon. His face had been so ghastly pale, the waxen pallor of the white shrouded form so terrifying, that M. Ingenbleek had recoiled at the sight of him, with the exclamation: "Oh, no, that is not the King. . . ." The doctors who carried out the autopsy were amazed at the condition of his arteries. Physically he could have lived to be a

Children cried with exhaustion; men who had left their workshops at six o'clock in the evening moved slowly along in the queue until six o'clock the following morning. Then, at last, they climbed the great flight of steps, passed into the *Chapelle Ardente,* paused a moment before the coffin for a last glimpse of their King. The spontaneous canonizations in the Middle Ages must have been like this, when the throngs of believers themselves elected the saints.

At eleven o'clock on the night before the funeral, shadows began to throng the pavements of the Rue Royale. The poor took up their positions by the Nadar Barrier. They shivered there all night long, like the refugees of 1914, while they waited for what was to pass. There was no unseemly noise, no disorder. Day broke, a sickly yellow dawn, and it began to drizzle. The people, who would do no work that day, had leaden circles under their eyes and were huddled together in utter exhaustion. At nine o'clock the coffin was brought out of the Palace and laid in an open space amidst a multitude of wreaths. Ex-soldiers filed past. Some of the most famous regiments of the War marched by, bareheaded and in civilian clothes, their gaze steady: no single word of command was given. The ninth of the Line, the twelfth of the Line, the Carabiniers, the Black Devils, made their appearance once more. Priests and peasants, workmen and lawyers, men from every sphere walked in the ranks. They kept step perfectly; and curés holding umbrellas over their heads

marched "eyes left" side by side with Generals in full uniform.

At eleven o'clock the bell of St. Jacques began to peal, a thin and mournful sound, like a village chime summoning the peasants to the burial of the lord of the manor. The sky was a dripping sponge. It was bitter cold. The last regiments passed by. The onlookers pressed against one another in jostling confusion—the one small disturbance of the day. When order had been restored, there was a stir at the entrance of the Palace. The crowd was wondering in what order the procession would issue forth. Would it be headed by a company of soldiers or by a standard-bearer? At that moment, three horsemen in long black cloaks, helmeted and gauntleted in black, rode out from the Palace on gigantic black thoroughbreds. The rider in the centre held aloft a standard swathed with crape. The crowd recognized them instantly: They were gendarmes of the historic escort, and the colours they bore were those of the 1914-1918 campaign. The people gazed at the Royal Flag of Brussels, Coorbeek-Loo, Battel, Antwerp, Selzaete, Eecloo, Ostend, La Panne, Lophem . . . the Pennon that had gone before their King in the sorrowful hours of disaster and retreat, the weary marches in the midst of his infantry, and on the triumphant to-morrows. The tinkling bell of St. Jacques continued to sound its mournful refrain. The gendarmes with the colours moved on slowly, with momentary pauses, as if they were figures in a dream; they were followed by archbishops and bishops in their ceremonial robes. And at last came the gun-carriage

that bore his coffin, seven feet long, draped with a flag. Behind walked a groom who led his horse, Titanic, in war-harness, the King's sword tied with crape hanging from the saddle.

The gun-carriage was drawn by the great men of the realm. I shall always carry a picture in my mind of the clear-cut features of M. Janson, the Minister of Justice. The rain fell unheeded on his bared head. The procession reached the steps of St. Gudule. Twelve non-commissioned officers of the Grenadiers lifted the coffin, and the gun-carriage continued on its way. Startled by this action the King's horse snorted, tossed his head in the rain, and reared wildly. The groom steadied him. With a long-drawn-out neigh, Titanic followed the gun-carriage through the midst of the heart-broken crowd. Princes, statesmen, admirals, field-marshals, ministers and generals entered the Cathedral. Meanwhile, the cortège had skirted the Park and turned the corner of the Rue de la Loi. Suddenly the branch of a tree crashed to the ground; several spectators were knocked down, and one was killed. No cry was uttered. The bell of St. Jacques had ceased to toll. It was still raining hopelessly.

The Princesses had driven to the Cathedral in carriages, but the crowd had not seen Queen Elisabeth, whose place in the procession was not set down in the official programme. A few privileged friends and a priest saw her step out of a car and steal into the church, shrouded in so long a veil that she was only a pathetic and mysterious shadow. The Belgian Princes and the Prince of Italy took their places on thrones ranged on

a crimson dais opposite the cardinals and bishops. Only
the carved marble figures of the Apostles stood out
against the dim tapestries. Behind the Prince of Wales
and President Lebrun were Pétain, Weygand, Brécard,
Allenby, Salmond, and the beloved Admiral Keyes;
veterans and survivors of the great battles; the disabled,
the blinded, the disfigured. The Requiem swept
through the Cathedral like the wind over the Yser, and
the sorrowful verses of the *Dies Irae* rose one by one
to Heaven.

The cortège formed for the return journey to Laeken.
The route lay through a vast faubourg, the Porte de
Bruxelles. Thousands of workmen clinging to scaffold-
ings made a high and murmurous hedge on either side
of the boulevard. King Boris of Bulgaria, one of the
mourners, said two days later in Berlin: "I saw the
strangest sight: men of the very poorest class clinging
to factory railings, weeping. . . ."

The Inniskilling Dragoons, their uniforms as close-
fitting as a dancer's tights, marched past at parade step,
their swords glittering. Next came the Chasseurs and
the French Marines with swinging step, headed by fife
and drum. Then followed a sea of flags, borne by ex-
soldiers, a heroic wave of colour. These regiments filed
past the new King and the Royal mourners, turned the
corner and disappeared from sight. The rain was
slackening.

Day brought comfort and peace. Twenty-five years
of devotion to duty were now to receive their crown.
After the obsequies, the Joyous Entry. The inaugura-

tion of the new reign took place amid rejoicing, though it lacked the presence of Queen Elisabeth. The young and handsome couple were well fitted to be the protagonists in this deeply moving pageant. The new Queen was soon to become a mother again. Seated between her two children, who were as lively as crickets, she drove round the capital in the state coach. The new King, followed by the Count of Flanders, rode to the Chamber on horseback, as his father had done before him, and delivered his speech with quiet dignity. His next action had no precedent: he mounted his horse and rode round the city, only pausing once—before the Tomb of the Unknown Soldier.

When the new King and Queen appeared on the balcony of the Palace in the dazzling sunlight, she in black, he in the uniform of a Lieutenant-General, the people, still subdued by the sorrow of the previous day, felt as though they were gazing at a reincarnation of the spirit of spring.

THE END

300
Jap